W9-DII-802

KNOLE AND THE SACKVILLES

RICHARD SACKVILLE, 3rd Earl of Dorset, 1589–1624

From the portrait by Daniel Mytens in the possession of Margaret Countess
of Suffolk and Berkshire

KNOLE

and

THE SACKVILLES

BY

V. SACKVILLE-WEST

LINDSAY DRUMMOND LIMITED
LONDON 1947

FIRST PUBLISHED NOVEMBER 1922
NEW EDITION   JANUARY 1923
REPRINTED   APRIL 1926
REPRINTED   FEBRUARY 1930
REPRINTED   JANUARY 1931
CHEAPER EDITION   1934
NEW EDITION   NOVEMBER 1947

Printed in Great Britain at Frome by
Butler & Tanner Limited

FOREWORD

to the reprint of 1947

THIS book was first published in 1922. Since it was written some new information has been incorporated in two massive volumes entitled *History of the Sackville Family, together with a description of Knole and early owners of Knole*, by Charles J. Phillips, published by Cassell & Co., Ltd., at eight guineas. Mr. Phillips, over a period of nearly ten years, undertook much original research at his own expense, employing readers to go through the manuscripts at Lambeth Palace, the Record Office, the British Museum, and the Diocesan Library at Canterbury ; personally investigating some of the contents of the Muniment Room at Knole ; and consulting such sources as the Pipe Rolls, the Charter Rolls, the Patent Rolls, the Close Rolls, and the reports of the Historical Manuscripts Commission. Had I possessed the common sense and patience to wait for the publication of Mr. Phillips's immense work, my own book would have been far more amply informed. But Mr. Phillips, so thorough and conscientious, was at the same time extremely dilatory and endearingly vague. He would lend me large lumps of his manuscript somewhat illegibly hand-written on foolscap paper, and never seemed to want them back. There were moments when I wondered whether his book would ever come out at all.

For these reasons I decided to go ahead with the publication of my own book, and now of course there are many alterations and additions I should like to

make. Unfortunately present conditions do not allow
a re-setting of the type ; the existing text has to be
reproduced by photolitho, and I must abide by what
I had written. In the interests of accuracy, however,
I here append a list of the major corrections I should
have wished to make ; some owing to Mr. Phillips,
some not :

(1) Page 5. There is no documentary evidence to
prove that Knole once belonged to the Earls of
Pembroke. The first known reference to Knole
occurs in the Lambeth Palace papers for 1281,
when it is found belonging to two unexplained
persons calling themselves William and Roger
de Knole.

(2) Page 8. Mr. Phillips quotes the account, given
by Cranmer's secretary, Ralph Morice, of the
circumstances leading to Cranmer's surrender
of Knole to Henry VIII :

> My Lord, minded to have retained Knole unto himself,
> said that it was too small a house for his Majesty. Marry, said
> the King, I had rather have it than this house, meaning
> Otford ; for it standeth on a better soil. This house standeth
> low, and is rheumatick, like unto Croydon, where I could
> never be without sickness. And as for Knole, it standeth on
> a sound, perfect, and wholesome ground ; and if I should
> make abode here, as I do surely mind to do now and then,
> I will live at Knole and most of my house shall live at Otford.
> And so by this means both those houses were delivered up
> into the King's hands.

(3) Page 15. An old tradition, which may be traced
back at least as far as Fanny Burney's letter to
her sister in October 1779, exists to the effect that
the furniture in the King's Bedroom was provided for the visit of James I. I meekly repeated
this statement (which is not contradicted by Mr.
Phillips) but now have good reason to suspect

its accuracy. For one thing, there is no mention of any visit to Knole in a detailed account of the Progresses of James I. This seems to me conclusive ; and there is the further argument that the sumptuous character of the carving and upholstery is suggestive of a later date.

Not all the silver in the King's Bedroom was made for Charles Sackville, 6th Earl of Dorset. Some of it, at any rate, belonged to his mother, Frances Cranfield. The silver table, for instance, has the monogram F. D. H. P. which Mr. Phillips interprets as meaning Frances Dorset and Henry Powle, her second husband.

It is also suggested (not by Mr. Phillips) that the silver furniture was copied from similar furniture made for Louis XIV at Versailles, all of which was melted down to meet some of the expense of war against England. The set at Knole would thus be the only one still in existence.

(4) Page 16. The tapestry in the Chapel was sold towards the payment of succession-duties in 1930, and now hangs in the Museum at Boston, Massachusetts.

(5) Page 20. Mr. Phillips remarks, without giving his authority, that the garden wall was built by the Lennards during a tenancy held by them of Knole in 1565.

(6) Page 152, line 6. For ' great-nephew ' read ' grandson '.

(7) Page 192. The Hoppner of the Three Children, like the tapestry in the Chapel, was sold towards the payment of succession-duties in 1930 and now hangs in the house of Mr. Thomas Lamont, New York.

Acknowledgements

My thanks are due to *Country Life* for the photographs of the Green Court, the Stone Court, the Venetian Ambassador's Bedroom, the Brown Gallery, the Leicester Gallery, and the Spangle Bedroom ; to Mr. Derek Adkins for the North-east view, the garden side, the Stone Court, the Cartoon Gallery, the Great Staircase, and the Great Hall ; to Messrs. George King, of Sevenoaks, for Lady Betty Germain's Bedroom, and the portraits of Lady Betty Germain, the 4th Earl of Dorset, his two sons, the 6th Earl of Dorset, Lady Anne Clifford, the 3rd Duke of Dorset, and the Three Children ; to the National Portrait Gallery for the *Somerset House Conference* 1604 ; to Aero Pictorial Ltd., for two air-photographs of Knole ; and to Margaret Countess of Suffolk and Berkshire for permission to reproduce the portrait of Richard, 3rd Earl of Dorset, by Daniel Mytens.

V. S.-W.

*Sissinghurst Castle, Kent
June 1947*

CHRONOLOGICAL TABLE

1281 First known reference to Knole, Lambeth Palace documents
1370 circa. Knole conveyed to GEOFFREY LORD DE SAY
1456 WILLIAM FIENNES, LORD SAYE AND SELE, great-great nephew
       of Geoffrey Lord de Say, sells Knole to THOMAS BOURCHIER,
       Archbishop of Canterbury
1486 Death of Bourchier. Succeeded by CARDINAL MORTON
1500 Death of Morton. Succeeded by HENRY DEANE
1503 Death of Deane. Succeeded by WILLIAM WARHAM
1532 Death of Warham. Succeeded by THOMAS CRANMER
1539 Knole given by Cranmer to HENRY VIII
1547 Death of Henry VIII. Succeeded by EDWARD VI
1551 Knole granted by Edward VI to DUDLEY, EARL OF WARWICK
       AND DUKE OF NORTHUMBERLAND
1553 Knole returned by Northumberland to EDWARD VI
1553 Death of Edward VI. Succeeded by QUEEN MARY
1556 Knole granted by Mary to REGINALD POLE
1558 Death of Mary. Death of Pole
1566 Knole granted to THOMAS SACKVILLE by QUEEN ELIZABETH

Thomas Sackville, LORD BUCKHURST, 1st EARL of DORSET, K.G., 1536–1608

1554 Married Cicely, daughter of Sir John Baker of Sissinghurst
       Castle, Cranbrook, Kent
1557}
1563} Member of Parliament
1563 Travelling abroad
1566 Death of his father, Sir Richard Sackville
1566 Given Knole by Queen Elizabeth
1567 Created Lord Buckhurst
1568}
1571} Ambassador to France
1569 Lord-Lieutenant of Sussex
1587}
1589} Ambassador to the Low Countries
1591 Chancellor of Oxford
1598 Ambassador to the Low Countries
1599 Lord High Treasurer
1601 Lord High Steward

1603 Death of Queen Elizabeth. Succeeded by JAMES I
1603 Lord Treasurer for life
1604 Created Earl of Dorset
1608 Death at the Council Table

Robert Sackville, 2nd EARL of DORSET, 1561–1609

1579 Married MARGARET HOWARD, daughter of 4th Duke of
     NORFOLK

1585⎱
1608⎰ Member of Parliament

1592 Married ANNE SPENCER
1608 Succeeded his father, THOMAS
1609 Death

Richard Sackville, 3rd EARL of DORSET, 1589–1624

1609 Married ANNE CLIFFORD, daughter of GEORGE, 3rd EARL OF
     CUMBERLAND
1609 Succeeded his father, ROBERT
1624 Death

Edward Sackville, 4th EARL of DORSET, K.G.,
1591–1652

1605 At Christ Church, Oxford
1612 Married MARY, daughter of SIR GEORGE CURZON
1614 His duel with LORD BRUCE
1614 Member of Parliament
1621 Ambassador to LOUIS XIII

1623⎱
1624⎰ Travels in Italy

1623 Again Ambassador to LOUIS XIII
1624 Succeeded his brother, RICHARD
1624 Lord-Lieutenant of Sussex and Middlesex
1625 Death of James I. Succeeded by CHARLES I
1628 Lord Chamberlain
1630 Lady Dorset appointed Governess to the King's children

1631⎱
1634⎰ Commissioner for Planting Virginia

1638 Granted the East Coast of America
1642 Outbreak of civil war. Lord Dorset joins the KING at York

1644   Lord Privy Seal
1649   Execution of CHARLES I
1652   Death

Richard Sackville, 5th EARL of DORSET, 1622–1677

1637   Married FRANCES CRANFIELD, daughterof LIONEL, EARL OF
        MIDDLESEX
1552   Succeeded his father, EDWARD
1670   Lord-Lieutenant of Sussex
1677   Death

Charles Sackville, 6th EARL of DORSET and EARL of MIDDLESEX, K.G., 1638–1706

1660   Member of Parliament
1660   Restoration of CHARLES II
1668   Ambassador to France
1674   Death of his mother ; he succeeds to the Cranfield estates
1675   Created EARL OF MIDDLESEX
1677   Succeeded his father, RICHARD, as EARL OF DORSET
1678   Married MARY, COUNTESS OF FALMOUTH
1685   Married MARY COMPTON, daughter of JAMES, EARL OF
        NORTHAMPTON
1685   Death of Charles II. Succeeded by JAMES II
1688   Accession of WILLIAM of ORANGE
1689
1697   Lord Chamberlain
1701   His poems published with SEDLEY's
1702   Death of William III. Succeeded by QUEEN ANNE
1704   Married ANNE ROCHE
1706   Death

Lionel Sackville, 7th EARL and 1st DUKE of DORSET, K.G., 1688–1765

1706   Succeeded his father, CHARLES, as EARL OF DORSET and
        MIDDLESEX
1709   Married ELIZABETH COLYEAR
1708   Lord Warden of the Cinque Ports, intermittently till 1728
1714   Death of Queen Anne. Succeeded by GEORGE I
1720   Created Duke of Dorset

1725 Lord Steward
1727 Death of George I. Succeeded by GEORGE II
1730 Lord-Lieutenant of Ireland till 1737
1746 Lord-Lieutenant of Kent
1750 Lord-Lieutenant of Ireland till 1755
1760 Death of George II. Succeeded by GEORGE III
1765 Death

Charles Sackville, 2nd DUKE of DORSET, 1711–1769

Before 1734. On the Grand Tour
1734 Member of Parliament intermittently till 1754. Lord of the Treasury and Master of the Horse
1744 Married GRACE BOYLE
1765 Succeeded his father, LIONEL
1769 Death

John Frederick Sackville, 3rd DUKE of DORSET, K.G., 1745–1799

1769 Succeeded his uncle, CHARLES
1783, 1789 Ambassador to LOUIS XVI
1769, 1797 Lord-Lieutenant of Kent
1789, 1799 Lord Steward
1790 Married ARABELLA DIANA, daughter of SIR JOHN COPE
1799 Death

George John Frederick Sackville, 4th DUKE of DORSET, 1794–1815

1799 Succeeded his father, JOHN FREDERICK
1815 Death

KNOLE FROM THE NORTH-EAST

Derek Adkins

THE GARDEN SIDE

TABLE OF DESCENT

HERBRAND DE SACKVILLE, *temp.* 𝖂illiam t𝖍e 𝕮onqueror

SIR RICHARD SACKVILLE, *temp.* 𝕳enrp VIII

THOMAS SACKVILLE *m. Cicely, dau. of Sir John Baker of Sissinghurst*
b. 1536   *d.* 1608
LORD BUCKHURST *and*
1st EARL *of* DORSET, K.G.
ROBERT SACKVILLE *m. Lady Margaret Howard*
b. 1561   *d.* 1609
2nd EARL *of* DORSET

RICHARD SACKVILLE *m.*   EDWARD SACKVILLE *m.*
        Lady Anne Clifford   *Mary Curzon*
b. 1589   *d.* 1624   *b.* 1589 *or* '90   *d.* 1652
3rd EARL *of* DORSET, K.G.   4th EARL *of* DORSET, K.G.

RICHARD SACKVILLE *m. Lady Frances Cranfield*
b. 1622 *d.* 1677, 5th EARL *of* DORSET
CHARLES SACKVILLE *m.* (1) *Mary Bagot*, (2) *Lady Mary Compton*, (3) *Anne Roche*
b. 1637 *or* '36   *d.* 1706
6th EARL *of* DORSET, K.G.

LIONEL SACKVILLE *m. Elizabeth Colyear*
b. 1686 *d.* 1765   [K.G.
7th EARL *and* 1st DUKE *of* DORSET,

CHARLES SACKVILLE   LORD JOHN SACKVILLE   LORD GEORGE SACKVILLE
b. 1711   *d* 1769   *d.* 1765   *b.* 1716   *d.* 1785
2nd DUKE *of* DORSET   *cr.* VISCOUNT SACKVILLE

JOHN FREDERICK SACKVILLE
m. Arabella Diana Cope   CHARLES SACKVILLE
b. 1745   *d.* 1799   *b.* 1767   *d.* 1843
3rd DUKE *of* DORSET, K.G.   5th DUKE *of* DORSET, K.G.

LADY MARY SACKVILLE   GEORGE JOHN FREDERICK SACKVILLE
m. (1) *the 6th Earl of Plymouth*   *b.* 1794 *d.* 1815 4th DUKE *of* DORSET
    (2) *William Pitt, Earl Amherst*   LADY ELIZABETH SACKVILLE
                                          m. John West, 5th Earl de la Warr
                                          b. 1796   *d.* 1870

CHARLES   MORTIMER   LIONEL   WILLIAM EDWARD
EARL DE LA WARR   1st LORD SACKVILLE   2nd LORD SACKVILLE
d. 1873   *b.* 1820 *d.* 1888 *b.* 1827 *d.* 1908 *b.* 1867 *d.* 1905

                        LIONEL   CHARLES
                   3rd LORD SACKVILLE   4th LORD SACKVILLE
                   b. 1867 *d.* 1930 *b.* 1870–

B

CONTENTS

LIST OF ILLUSTRATIONS

The dome of Knole, by fame enrolled,
   The Church of Canterbury,
The hops, the beer, the cherries there,
   Would fill a noble story.

CHAPTER I

The House

§ i

THERE are two sides from which you may first profitably look at the house. One is from the park, the north side. From here the pile shows best the vastness of its size; it looks like a mediaeval village. It is heaped with no attempt at symmetry ; it is sombre and frowning ; the grey towers rise; the battlements cut out their square regularity against the sky; the buttresses of the old twelfth-century tithe-barn give a rough impression of fortifications. There is a line of trees in one of the inner courtyards, and their green heads show above the roofs of the old breweries ; but although they are actually trees of a considerable size they are dwarfed and unnoticeable against the mass of the buildings blocked behind them. The whole pile soars to a peak which is the clock-tower with its pointed roof: it might be the spire of the church on the summit of the hill crowning the mediaeval village. At sunset I have seen the silhouette of the great building stand dead black on a red sky; on moonlight nights it stands black and silent, with glinting windows, like an enchanted castle. On misty autumn nights I have seen it emerging partially from the trails of vapour, and heard the lonely roar of the red deer roaming under the walls.

§ ii

The other side is the garden side—the gay, princely side, with flowers in the foreground; the grey walls rising straight up from the green turf; the mullioned

1

windows, and the Tudor gables with the heraldic leopards sitting stiffly at each corner. The park side is the side for winter; the garden side the side for summer. It has an indescribable gaiety and courtliness. The grey of the Kentish rag is almost pearly in the sun, the occasional coral festoon of a climbing rose dashed against it; the long brown-red roofs are broken by the chimney-stacks with their slim, peaceful threads of blue smoke mounting steadily upwards. One looks down upon the house from a certain corner in the garden. Here is a bench among a group of yews—dark, red-berried yews; and the house lies below one in the hollow, lovely in its colour and its serenity. It has all the quality of peace and permanence ; of mellow age ; of stateliness and tradition. It is gentle and venerable. Yet it is, as I have said, gay. It has the deep inward gaiety of some very old woman who has always been beautiful, who has had many lovers and seen many generations come and go, smiled wisely over their sorrows and their joys, and learnt an imperishable secret of tolerance and humour. It is, above all, an English house. It has the tone of England ; it melts into the green of the garden turf, into the tawnier green of the park beyond, into the blue of the pale English sky; it settles down into its hollow amongst the cushioned tops of the trees; the brown-red of those roofs is the brown-red of the roofs of humble farms and pointed oast-houses, such as stain over a wide landscape of England the quilt-like pattern of the fields. I make bold to say that it stoops to nothing either pretentious or meretricious. There is here no flourish of archi-tecture, no ornament but the leopards, rigid and vigilant. The stranger may even think, upon arrival, that the front of the house is disappointing. It is, indeed, extremely modest. There is a gate-house flanked by two square grey towers, placed between two wings which provide only a monotony of windows and gables. It is true that two or three fine sycamores, symmetrical and circular as open umbrellas, redeem the severity of the front, and that a herd of fallow deer, browsing in the dappled shade of the trees, maintains the tradition of an English park. But, for the rest, the front of the house is so severe as to be positively uninteresting; it is quiet and monkish; " a beautiful decent simplicity," said Horace Walpole, " which charms one." There is here to be found none of the splendour of Elizabethan building. A different impression, however, is in store when once the wicket-gate has been opened. You are in a courtyard of a size the frontage had never led you to expect, and the vista through a second gateway shows you the columns of a second court ; your eye is caught by an oriel window opposite, and by other windows with heraldic bearings in their panes, promise of rooms and galleries ; by gables and the heraldic leopards; by the clock tower which gives an oddly Chinese effect immediately above the Tudor oriel. Up till a few years ago Virginia creeper blazed scarlet in autumn on the walls of the Green Court, but it has now been torn away, and what may be lost in colour is compensated by the gain in seeing the grey stone and the slight moulding which runs, following the shape of the towers, across the house.

On the whole, the quadrangle is reminiscent of Oxford, though more palatial and less studious. The house is built round a system of these courtyards: first this one, the Green Court, which is the largest and most magnificent; then the second one, or Stone Court, which is not turfed, like the Green Court, but wholly paved, and which has along one si of it a Jacobean colonnade ; the third court is the Water Court, and has none of the display of the first t o : it is smaller, and quite demure, indeed rather like ome old house in Nuremberg, with the latticed win ow of one of the galleries running the whole len h of it, and the friendly unconcern of an immen bay-tree growing against one of its walls. There are four other courts, making seven in all. This number is supposed to correspond to the days in the week ; and in pursuance of this conceit there are in the house fifty-two staircases, corresponding to the weeks in the year, and three hundred and sixty-five rooms, corresponding to the days. I cannot truthfully pretend that I have ever verified these counts, and it may be that their accuracy is accepted solely on the strength of the legend; but, if this is so, then it has been a very persistent legend, and I prefer to sympathise with the amusement of the ultimate architect on making the discovery that by a judicious juggling with his additions he could bring courts, stairs, and rooms up to that satisfactory total.

A stone lobby under the oriel window divides the Green Court from the Stone Court. In summer the great oak doors of this second gate-house are left open, and it has sometimes happened that I have found a stag in the banqueting hall, puzzled but still dignified, strayed in from the park since no barrier checked him.

It becomes impossible, after passing through the formality of the two first quadrangles, to follow the ramblings of the house geographically. They are so involved that, after a lifetime of familiarity, I still catch myself pausing to think out the shortest route from one room to another. Four acres of building is no mean matter.

§ iii

Into the very early mediaeval history of the house I do not think that I need enter. It is suggested that a Roman building once occupied the site, and that some foundations which were recently unearthed beneath the larder—evidently one of the oldest portions—once formed part of that construction. The question of dating the existing buildings, however, is quite sufficiently complicated without going back to a building which no longer exists. Nor do I think that the early owners—the Pembrokes, or the Say and Seles—offer the smallest interest ; if we knew precisely what parts of the house we owed to them severally it would be another matter, but the mediaeval records are very scanty. It is safe to say, generally speaking, that the north side is the oldest side ; it is the most sombre, the most massive, and the most irregular; there are buttresses, battlements, and towers, but no gables and no embellishments—nothing but solid masonry. Up in the north-east corner is the old kitchen, and the old entrances through dark archways at the top of stairways. The passages here, of thick stone, twist oddly, and their ceilings are groined by semi-arches which have become lost and embedded in the alterations to the stone-work. It is a dark, massive, little-visited corner, this nucleus of Knole.

The house, or such portions of it as then existed, was bought from William, Lord Say and Sele, by Bourchier, Archbishop of Canterbury, on June 30, 1456, and it is clear from the numerous bills among the archives at Lambeth Palace that both he and his more notable successor, Cardinal Morton, carried out extensive additions, alterations, and repairs. It is, however, a very difficult task to determine what parts of the building definitely belong to this period, for, what with the additions of the archbishops and the alterations of the later Sackvilles, all is confusion. It would appear, for instance, that upon a foundation of Tudor masonry the Sackvilles constructed the Elizabethan gables which are now so characteristic a feature of the house; but it is less easy to say exactly how much the first Tudor archbishop found there on his arrival of earlier workmanship. A further confusing factor is the great fire which took place in 1623, and is reported to have destroyed a large part of the building—but exactly where, and how much, we cannot say. Nor are the accounts at Lambeth very illuminating :

In divers costs and expenses made this year [1467] for repairing the manor of Knole, carriage for the two cart loads of lathes from Panters to the manor, 14*d*. For carriage of thirty loads of stone for the new tower, 7*d*. load = 16/9. Carriage of six loads of timber at 7*d*. = 3/6. Carriage of one fother of lead from London to Knole, 3/4.

The next year, 1468 :

Repairs at Knole. One labourer for 6 days work in the great chamber and the new *seler*, 2/–. Making of 700 lathes to the new tower, 14*d*. One labourer 4½ days in the old kitchen, 4*d*. Item, for 1 j M¹ of walle prygge (*sic*) to the stable and other places, 13*d*. One cowl to the masonry, 12*d*.

The " great chamber " referred to here was in all probability the present Great Hall, which we know to have been built by Bourchier about 1460, although it was altered by Thomas Sackville, who put in the present ceiling, panelling, and oak screen. Thomas also built the Great Staircase in 1604–8, leading to the Ballroom, which is of the time of Bourchier. I expect this is the " seler " referred to, meaning solar and not cellar, as might be thought ; or did it mean the present colonnade, which is also of Bourchier's building, in 1468 ? The position of the " new tower " is nowhere specified, but I wonder whether it is not the tower beside the chapel, where there is a stone fireplace bearing Bourchier's cognisance—the double knot—and the same device in a small pane of stained glass in the window. This tower, moreover, goes commonly by the name of Bourchier's Tower.

There are a few more items mentioned in the Lambeth papers, 1468-9 : " Repairs at Knole. Repairs at one house set aside for the slaughter of sheep and other [animals ?] for the use of the Lord's great house at Sevenoaks, 11 3s. 2d." This, I think, is certainly the old slaughter-house which forms one side of the Queen's Court. It is obviously a very old building. But there is one point in this account which is of interest, namely, that Knole should at this date have been referred to as the " great house." This would seem to prove that the greater mass of the building was already in existence, since by the latter half of the fifteenth century there were already many houses and palaces in England whose bulk would argue that the current standard of greatness might be high and the adjective not too readily applied. The Primate owned, moreover, up to the time of the Reformation no less than twelve palaces and houses of residence in the diocese of Canterbury alone, namely, Bekesburn, Ford, Maidstone, Charing, Saltwood, Aldington, Wingham, Wrotham, Tenterden, Knole, Otford, and Canterbury. It seems, therefore, unlikely that Knole should be singled out as a " great house " unless there were good justification for the expression.

Bourchier also built the Brown Gallery about 1460,

and at or about the same date he put up the machicolations over the gate-house between the Green Court and the Stone Court. Towards the end of the same century, Morton, his successor, " threw out an oriel window which rendered the machicolations useless, and showed that all idea of such fortifications was at an end." It is not known precisely how much Morton built at Knole. It is even uncertain whether he or Bourchier built the Chapel. The Lambeth records cease with some small repairs in 1487–88, so we have nothing to go upon—all the more pity, for Morton was a great prelate, forgotten now in the greater fame of the Tudor dynasty, " his name buried," says his chronicler, " under his own creation." This cardinal, having succeeded Bourchier in 1486, held the Primacy for fourteen years, and died at Knole in 1500. I pass over his successors, Dean and Wareham, for I do not know how much they did at Knole. Cranmer, the next archbishop, enjoyed the house for seven years only, when he was compelled—quite amicably, but nevertheless compelled—to present it to Henry VIII, whose fancy it had taken. Here the accounts begin again,[1] although they give very little indication: £872 by Royal Warrant in 1543, £770 in 1548, £80 in 1546—three sums which would now be equivalent, roughly, to £30,000.

After Henry VIII Knole continued as Crown property, passing now and then temporarily into the hands of various favourites, until in 1586 it was given by Queen Elizabeth to her cousin, Thomas Sackville, and has remained in the possession of his family ever since.

[1] State papers of Henry VIII.

8

§ iv

The main block, therefore, meanders from Henry
VII through Henry VIII to Elizabeth and James I :
that is to say, roughly, from the end of the fifteenth
century to the beginning of the seventeenth. There
may be earlier out-buildings and later excrescences,
but it is safe to say that the greater portion was built
in the reigns of the Tudors. It is all of the same
Kentish rag, with the exception of a row of gables
which have been plastered over, and which were probably once of the beam-and-plaster fashion so prevalent
at that date in Kent. With this exception the walls are
of the grey stone, in many places ten and twelve feet
thick, cool in summer, and, for some reason, not particularly warm in winter. The rooms are, for the most
part, rather small and rather low ; they break out, of
course, now into galleries, now into a ball-room, now
into a banqueting-hall, but the majority of them are
small, friendly rooms—not intimidating ; some people
might even think them poky, relative to the size of the
house. I do not think that they are poky. They are
eminently rooms intended to be lived in, and not
merely admired, though no doubt a practical consideration was present in the problem of heating to
determine their size. Yet from an old diary preserved
at Knole, and from which in its place I shall have the
opportunity to give extracts, it is clear that in the
early seventeenth century at all events the life of the
house was carried on largely in one or the other of the
long galleries. Now, none of the galleries has more than
one fireplace. It must have been very cold. The old
braziers that could be carried about the room as
occasion required still stand in the rooms where they

were used, and so do the copper warming-pans, shining and perforated, which were thrust into the beds to warm them before the arrival of the occupant. The principal beds, of course, must have been magnificently stuffy. They are four-posters, so tall as to reach from floor to ceiling, with stiff brocaded curtains that could completely enclose the sleeper. But on winter days I cannot believe that the group ever moved very far away from the fireplace or the brazier; and indeed, judging from the same diary, they seemed always to be " keeping their chamber " on account of coughs, colds, rheumatism, or ague when they were not keeping it because they were " sullen " with one another, or " brought to bed " of a son or a daughter.

§ v

The galleries are perhaps the most characteristic rooms in such a house.

Long and narrow, with dark shining floors, armorial glass in the windows, rich plasterwork ceilings, and portraits on the walls, they are splendidly sombre and sumptuous. The colour of the Cartoon Gallery, when I have come into it in the evening, with the sunset flaming through the west window, has often taken my breath away. I have stood, stock still and astonished, in the doorway. The gallery is ninety feet in length, the floor formed of black oak planks irregularly laid, the charm of which is that they are not planks at all, but solid tree-trunks, split in half, with the rounded half downwards ; and on this oak flooring lie the blue and scarlet patches from the stained west window, more subduedly echoed in the velvets of the chair coverings, the coloured marbles of the great Renaissance fire-

place, and the fruits and garlands of the carved woodwork surrounding the windows. There is nothing
garish : all the colours have melted into an old
harmony that is one of the principal beauties of these
rooms. The walls here in the Cartoon Gallery are hung
with rose-red Genoa velvet, so lovely that I almost
regret Mytens' copies of the Raphael cartoons hiding
most of it ; but if, at Knole, one were too nicely
reluctant to sacrifice the walls, whether panelled or
velvet-hung, then all the pictures would have to be
stacked on the floor of the attics. The same regret
applies to the ball-room, where the Elizabethan
panelling—oak, but originally painted white, turned
by age to ivory—is so covered up as to be unnoticeable
behind the Sackville portraits of ten generations.
Fortunately, the frieze in the ball-room cannot be
hidden. It used to delight me as a child, with its carved
intricacies of mermaids and dolphins, mermen and
mermaids with scaly, twisting tails and salient anatomy,
and I was invariably contemptuous of those visitors to
whom I pointed out the frieze but who were more
interested in the pictures. It always fell to my lot to
" show the house " to visitors when I was living there
alone with my grandfather, for he shared the family
failing of unsociability, and whenever a telegram
arrived threatening invasion he used to take the next
train to London for the day, returning in the evening
when the coast was clear. It mattered nothing that
I was every whit as bored by the invasion as he could
have been ; in a divergence between the wishes of
eighty and the wishes of eight, the wishes of eight
went to the wall.

§ vi

There are other galleries, older and more austere than the Cartoon Gallery. They are not quite so long, they are narrower, lower, and darker, and not so exuberant in decoration ; indeed, they are simply and soberly panelled in oak. They have the old, musty smell which, to me, whenever I met it, would bring back Knole. I suppose it is really the smell of all old houses—a mixture of woodwork, pot-pourri, leather, tapestry, and the little camphor bags which keep away the moth ; the smell engendered by the shut windows of winter and the open windows of summer, with the breeze of summer blowing in from across the park. Bowls of lavender and dried rose-leaves stand on the window-sills ; and if you stir them up you get the quintessence of the smell, a sort of dusty fragrance, sweeter in the under layers where it has held the damp of the spices. The pot-pourri at Knole is always made from the recipe of a prim-looking little old lady who lived there for many years as a guest in the reigns of George I and George II. Her two rooms open out of one of the galleries, two of the smallest rooms in the house, the bedroom hung with a pale landscape of blue-green tapestry, the sitting-room panelled in oak ; and in the bedroom stands her small but pompous bed, with bunches of ostrich-plumes nodding at each of the four corners. Strangers usually seem to like these two little rooms best, coming to them as they do, rather overawed by the splendour of the galleries ; they are amused by the smallness of the four-poster, square as a box, its creamy lining so beautifully quilted; by the spinning-wheel, with the shuttle still full of old flax; and by the ring-box, containing a number of plain-cut

KNOLE FROM THE AIR

THE GREEN COURT

stones, which could be exchanged at will into the single gold setting provided. The windows of these rooms, furthermore, look out on to the garden ; they are human, habitable little rooms, reassuring after the pomp of the Ball-room and the galleries. In the sitting-room there is a small portrait of the prim lady, Lady Betty Germaine, sitting very stiff in a blue brocaded dress ; she looks as though she had been a martinet in a tight, narrow way.

The gallery leading to these rooms is called the Brown Gallery. It is well named—oak floor, oak walls, and barrelled ceiling, criss-crossed with oak slats in a pattern something like cat's cradle. Some of the best pieces of the English furniture are ranged down each side of this gallery : portentously important chairs, Jacobean cross-legged or later love-seats in their original coverings, whether of plum and silver, or red brocade with heavy fringes, or green with silver fringes, or yellow silk sprigged in black, or powder-blue ; and all have their attendant stool squatting beside them. They are lovely, silent rows, for ever holding out their arms, and for ever disappointed. At the end of this gallery is a tiny oratory, down two steps, for the use of the devout : this little, almost secret, place glows with colour like a jewel, but nobody ever notices it, and on the whole it probably prefers to hide itself away unobserved.

There is also the Leicester Gallery, which preserves in its name the sole trace of Lord Leicester's brief owner-ship of Knole. The Leicester Gallery is very dark and mysterious, furnished with red velvet Cromwellian farthingale chairs and sofas, dark as wine ; there are illuminated scrolls of two family pedigrees—Sackville and Curzon—richly emblazoned with coats of arms, drawn out in 1589 and 1623 respectively ; and in the end window there is a small stained-glass portrait of "Herbrand de Sackville, a Norman notable, came into England with William the Conqueror, A.D. 1066." (*Herbrandus de Sackville, Praepotens Normanus, intravit Angliam cum Gulielmo Conquestore, Anno Domini MLXVI.*) There is also a curious portrait hanging on one of the doors, of Catherine Fitzgerald Countess of Desmond, the portrait of a very old lady, in a black dress and a white ruff, with that strange far-away look in her dead blue eyes that comes with extreme age. For tradition says of her that she was born in the reign of Edward the Fourth and died in the reign of Charles the First, breaking her leg incidentally at the age of ninety by falling off a cherry tree ; that is to say, she was a child when the princes were smothered in the Tower, a girl when Henry the Seventh came to the throne, and watched the pageant of all the Tudors and the accession of the Stuarts—the whole of English history enclosed between the Wars of the Roses and the Civil War. She must have been a truly legendary figure in the country by the time she had reached the age of a hundred and forty or there-abouts.

It is rather a frightening portrait, that portrait of Lady Desmond. If you go into the gallery after night-fall with a candle the pale, far-away eyes stare past you into the dark corners of the wainscot, eyes either over-charged or empty—which ? The house is not haunted, but you require either an unimaginative nerve or else a complete certainty of the house's benevolence before you can wander through the state-rooms after nightfall with a candle. The light gleams on the dull gilding of furniture and into the misty depths of mirrors, and startles up a sudden face out of the gloom ; something creaks and sighs ; the tapestry sways, and the figures on it undulate and seem to come alive. The recesses of the great beds, deep in shadow, might be inhabited, and you would not know it ; eyes might watch you, unseen. The man with the candle is under a terrible disadvantage to the man in the dark.

§ vii

As there are three galleries among the state-rooms, so are there three principal bedrooms : the King's, the Venetian Ambassador's, and the Spangled Room. The King's bedroom is the only vulgar room in the house. Not that the furniture put there for the reception of James the First is vulgar : it is excessively magnificent, the canopy of the immense bed reaching almost to the ceiling, decked with ostrich feathers, the hangings stiff with gold and silver thread, the coverlet and the interior of the curtains heavily embroidered with a design of pomegranates and tiger-lilies worked in silver on a coral satin ground, the royal cipher embossed over the pillows—all this is very magnificent, but not vulgar. What is vulgar is the set of furniture made entirely in silver : table, hanging mirror, and tripods—the florid and ostentatious product of the florid Restoration. There is a surprising amount of silver in the room : sconces, ginger-jars, mirrors, fire-dogs, toilet-set, rose-water sprinklers, even to a little eye-bath, all of silver, but these smaller objects have not the blatancy of the set of furniture. Charles Sackville, for whom it was made, cannot have known when he had had enough of a good thing.

It is almost a relief to go from here to the Venetian Ambassador's Bedroom. Green and gold ; Burgundian tapestry, mediaeval figures walking in a garden ; a rosy Persian rug—of all rooms I never saw a room that so had over it a bloom like the bloom on a bowl of grapes and figs. I cannot keep the simile, which may convey nothing to those who have not seen the room, out of my mind. Greens and pinks originally bright, now dusted and tarnished over. It is a very grave, stately room, rather melancholy in spite of its stateliness. It seems to miss its inhabitants more than do any of the other rooms. Perhaps this is because the bed appears to be designed for three : it is of enormous breadth, and there are three pillows in a row. Presumably this is what the Italians call a *letto matrimoniale.*

§ viii

In a remote corner of the house is the Chapel of the Archbishops, small, and very much bejewelled. Tapestry, oak, and stained-glass—the chapel smoulders with colour. It is greatly improved since the oak has been pickled and the mustard-yellow paint removed, also the painted myrtle-wreaths, tied with a gilt ribbon, in the centre of each panel, with which the nineteenth century adorned it, when it was considered " very simple, plain, and neat in its appearance, and well adapted for family worship." The hand of the nineteenth century fell rather heavily on the chapel : besides painting the oak yellow and the ceiling blue with gold stars, it erected a Gothic screen and a yellow organ ; but fortunately these are both at the entrance, and you can turn your back on them and look down the little nave to the altar where Mary Queen of Scots' gifts stand under the Perpendicular east window. All along the left-hand wall hangs the Gothic tapestry—

scenes from the life of Christ, the figures, ungainly enough, trampling on an edging of tall irises and lilies exquisitely designed ; and " Saint Luke in his first profession," wrote Horace Walpole irreverently, " holding a urinal." There used to be other tapestries in the house ; there was one of the Seven Deadly Sins set, woven with gold threads, and there was another series, very early, representing the Flood and the two-by-two procession of the animals going into a weather-boarded Ark ; but these, alas, had to be sold, and are now in America.

The chapel looks strange and lovely during a midnight thunderstorm : the lightning flashes through the stone ogives of the east window, and one gets a queer effect, unreal like colour photography, of the colours lit up by that unfamiliar means. A flight of little private steps leads out of my bedroom straight into the Family Pew ; so I dare to say that there are few aspects under which I have not seen the chapel ; and as a child I used to " take sanctuary " there when I had been naughty : that is to say, fairly often. They never found me, sulking inside the pulpit.

§ ix

There would, of course, be many other aspects from which I might consider Knole ; indeed, if I allowed myself full licence I might ramble out over Kent and down into Sussex, to Lewes, Buckhurst, and Withyham, out into the fruit country and the hop country, across the Weald, over Saxonbury, and to Lewes among the Downs, and still I should not feel guilty of irrelevance. Of whatever English county I spoke, I still should be aware of the relationship between the

17

English soil and that most English house. But more especially do I feel this concerning Kent and Sussex, and concerning the roads over which the Sackvilles travelled so constantly between estate and estate. The place-names in their letters recur through the centuries ; the paper is a little yellower as the age increases, the ink a little more faded, the handwriting a little less easily decipherable, but still the gist is always the same: " I go to-morrow into Kent," " I quit Buckhurst for Knole," " my Lord rode to Lewes with a great company," " we came to Knole by coach at midnight." The whole district is littered with their associations, whether a village whose living lay in their gift, or a town where they endowed a college, or a wood where they hunted, or the village church where they had themselves buried. Sussex, in fact, was their cradle long before they came into Kent. Buckhurst, which they had owned since the twelfth century, was at one time an even larger house than Knole, and to their own vault in its parish church of Withyham they were invariably brought to rest. Their trace is scattered over the two counties. But this was not my only meaning ; I had in mind that Knole was no mere excrescence, no alien fabrication, no startling stranger seen between the beeches and the oaks. No other country but England could have produced it, and into no other country would it settle with such harmony and such quiet. The very trees have not been banished from the courtyards, but spread their green against the stone. From the top of a tower one looks down upon the acreage of roofs, and the effect is less that of a palace than of a jumbled village upon the hillside. It is not an incongruity like Blenheim or Chatsworth, foreign to the spirit of England. It is, rather, the greater relation of those small manor-houses which hide themselves away so innumerably among the counties, whether built of the grey stone of south-western England, or the brick of East Anglia, or merely tile-hung or plastered like the cottages. It is not utterly different from any of these. The great Palladian houses of the eighteenth century are *in* England, they are not *of* England, as are these irregular roofs, this easy straying up the contours of the hill, these cool coloured walls, these calm gables, and dark windows mirroring the sun.

CHAPTER II

The Garden and Park

§ i

YOU come out of the cool shadowy house on to the warm garden, in the summer, and there is a scared flutter of white pigeons up to the roof as you open the door. You have to look twice before you are sure whether they are pigeons or magnolias. The turf is of the most brilliant green; there is a sound of bees in the limes ; the heat quivers like watered gauze above the ridge of the lawn. The garden is entirely enclosed by a high wall of rag, very massively built, and which perhaps dates back to the time of the archbishops ; its presence, I think, gives a curious sense of seclusion and quiet. Inside the walls are herbaceous borders on either side of long green walks, and little square orchards planted with very old apple-trees, under which grow iris, snapdragon, larkspur, pansies, and such-like humble flowers. There are also interior walls, with rounded archways through which one catches a sight of the house, so that the garden is conveniently divided up into sections without any loss of the homogeneity of the whole. Half of the garden, roughly speaking, is formal; the other half is woodland, called the Wilderness, mostly of beech and chestnut, threaded by mossy paths which in spring are thick with bluebells and daffodils.

The old engravings show the gardens to have been, from the seventeenth century onwards, very much the same as they are at present. There are a few minor variations, but as the early engravers were not very particular as to accuracy their evidence cannot be accepted as wholly reliable. We have, besides these engravings, a fairly large number of records relating to both the park and gardens. The earliest of these that I have been able to trace is dated 1456, to the effect that Archbishop Bourchier in that year enclosed the park—a smaller area then than is covered by it now; and in 1468 there is a bill, " Paid for making 1000 palings for the enclosure of the Knole land, 6s. 8d." But the first accounts for the garden proper appear to date from the reign of Henry VIII (State papers of Henry VIII), when, in 1543, Sir Richard Longe was paid " for making the King's garden at Knole." Then there is a gap of nearly a century, save for the references to the garden in Lady Anne Clifford's Diary, such as " 25th October, 1617. My Lady Lisle and my Coz: Barbara Sidney [came ?] and I walked with them all the Wilderness over. They saw the Child and much commended her. I gave them some marmalade of quince, for about this time I made much of it"; and her constant notes of how she took her prayer-book " up to the standing " [which I take to be what we now call the Duchess' Seat], or of how she picked cherries in the garden with the French page, and he told her how he thought that all the men in the house loved her. For the year 1692, however, there are some bills among the Knole papers, such as " Mr. Olloynes, gardener, wages £12 per annum," and some bills for seeds and roots, " Sweet yerbs, pawsley, sorrill, spinnig, spruts, leeks, sallet, horse-rydish, jerusalem hawty-chorks," and another bill for seeds for £2. 0s. 5d. Coming to the eighteenth century, there are more detailed accounts, amongst others an agreement of what was expected in those days of a head gardener and the remuneration he might hope to receive :

14th Aug., 1706. Ric. Baker, Gardener with Lionel Earl of Dorset and Middlesex. To serve his Lordship as Gardener at Knole for the term of one year ½ to begin in March 1706. That he will reserve all the fruit which shall be growing in the garden for his Lordship's use. That he will at his own charge during the said term preserve all Trees and Greens now in the garden, and will maintain the trees in good husbandlike manner by pruning and trimming, dunging and marling the same in seasonable times, and likewise at his own charge will provide all herbs and other things convenient for my Lord's kitchen there when in season. He undertakes to maintain at his own charge all such walks as are now in ye said Garden, by mowing, cleaning, and rolling the same, and will preserve all such flowers and plants as are now in the gardens, and that he will be at all the charges of repairing all the glass frames, etc. belonging to the Garden Trade, and will provide for the present use of the Gardens 50 loads of dung.

In return for this service he was to be allowed £30 per annum, and

rooms and conveniences in the house for his business, and to hand all such dung, etc. as shall be made about the house for the use of ye gardens, and that he may have the privilege of disposing [for his own use] all such beans, peas, cabbages, and other kitchen herbs as shall be spared, over and above that what is used in my Lord's kitchen.

April 28, 1718.

	£	s.	d.
Planting trees in new Oak Walk, 5 men, 8 to 18 days each	3	12	4
Planting walnut trees round the Keeper's lodge, 3 men, 5 days each at 1/2 each per day	0	17	6
Cutting Bows in the yew at end of new Oak Walk	0	2	4

November 11, 1723.

Cutting and levelling new walk in ye Wilder-

	£	s.	d
ness and making ye mount round ye Oak tree, 8 men, 5 to 11 days each	3	10	0
Alterations made in the Fruit Walks, 16 men, from 14 to 43 days each	23	19	10
Cutting 10,600 turfs at 8*d.* per 100	3	10	8
Planting ye quarry in the Park	6	7	0
10 May Duke Cherries in ye garden	0	6	8
6 peach and nectarine trees in ye garden	0	12	0
2400 quick-set for ye kitchen garden	0	12	0
1000 holly for ye kitchen garden	0	10	0
Planting 2000 small beeches in ye park	0	18	6
200 Pear stocks	0	6	0
300 Crab stocks	0	3	0
200 Cherry stocks	0	6	0
500 Holly stocks	0	5	0
700 Hazel stocks	1	15	0
For new making the Mulberry garden and sowing ye front walk with seed	14	12	9
20 Gascon Cherry trees	0	10	0
50 bushels sweet apples for cyder	2	10	0
1 bushel Buckwheat for ye Pheasants	0	3	6
10,000 seedling beeches for my Lady Germaine	0	10	0

December 24, 1726.

	£	s.	d
Getting 80 load of ice and putting it in ye Ice House	1	15	3

June 15, 1728.

	£	s.	d
Planting 160 Elms in field which was Dr. Lambarde's next Tonbridge road and sowing the field with furze seed	7	9	3

April, 1730.

	£	s.	d
1000 Asparagus plants from Gravesend	1	0	0
2 doz. Apricots	0	2	0
300 beeches 8ft. high	1	15	0
250 large beeches planted in ye Park	3	10	0

It is not very clear where such a large number of fruit trees were to be used, but on an engraving of about 1720 I find a wall extending right across the garden to the two stone pillars which, surmounted by carved stone urns, still remain, this wall being planted with fruit trees, so I should think it very probable that this would account for it.

In 1777 new hot-houses and " Pineries " were built, and £175 paid for " two hot-houses full stocked with pine apples and plants."

§ ii

Surrounding the house and gardens lies the park, with its valleys, hills, and woods, and its short brown turf closely bitten by deer and rabbits. Its beeches and bracken, its glades and valleys, greatly excited the admiration of Mrs. Ann Radcliffe, who visited it in the beginning of the nineteenth century, and she wrote with enthusiasm of shade rising above shade with *amazing* and *magnificent* grandeur, and of one beech in particular spreading "its light yet umbrageous fan " over a seat placed round the bole. With all its grandeur and luxuriance, she said, there was nothing about this beech heavy or formal ; it was airy, though vast and majestic, and suggested an idea at once of the *strength* and *fire* of a *hero*. She would call a beech tree, she added, and this beech above every other, the hero of the forest, as the oak was called the king.

As I have said, the park was first enclosed by Bourchier in 1456, the year in which he bought Knole on the 30th of June. In the muniments at Lambeth are a number of papers relating to the expenses of this great builder, and there is the interesting fact that glass-making was carried on in the park, and I only wish that more detailed accounts existed of this industry, which, thanks to the Huguenots, had been pretty widely introduced into the South of England. I should like to know exactly where their glass-foundry was, and whether they made use of the sand on the portion known as the Furze-field, now a rabbit warren; and I should also very much like to know whether—as seems probable—they supplied any of the glass for the windows in the house.

It would appear that the park, now entirely under grass, was once ploughland, for there is at Knole a deed of the time of Richard Sackville, fifth Earl of Dorset— that is to say, the middle of the seventeenth century— which accords to four farmers " the liberty to plough anywhere in the Park except in the plain set out by my Lord and the ground in front of the house, and to take three crops, and it is agreed that one-third of each crop after it is severed from the ground shall be taken and carried away by my Lord for his own use. The third year, the farmers to sow the ground with grass seed if my Lord desires it, and they are to be at the charge of the seed, the tillage, and the harvest." Later on, in the time of Charles I, hops were grown, not only around the park, but also in it. Women employed in picking the hops were paid 5d. a day, but for cleaning and weeding the ground they only received 3d. At this time also cattle were fed in the park during the summer, and belonging to the same date (about 1628) are the bills for " Moles caught, 1½d. each "; " Mowing the meadows," at the rate of 1s. 6d. per acre ; " Making hay," also at 1s. 6d. per acre ; " Carriage of hay from the meadows to Knole barn," 1s. 4d. per load : " one hay fork and 2 hay forks together,"

1*s*. 8*d*. For " hunting conies by night and ferret by day " 4*s*. was paid ; the expenses involved by the "conies" for one year were exactly £10, which included £5 5*s*., a year's wages for the " wariner "; but, on the other hand, this was money well expended, for the revenue from " conies sold " covers no less than a fifth part of the year's total income. The " wariner," although his £5 5*s*. a year hardly seems excessive, did better than the " wood-looker," who, for his woodreeveship for a year, was paid only £2.

The accounts of how and when the various outlying portions of the park were taken in can only be of local interest, and I do not therefore propose to go into them. They were mostly bought by John Frederick, the third duke, and by Lord Whitworth, who had married John Frederick's widow. The ruins round the queer little sham Gothic house called the Bird House —which always frightened me as a child because I thought it looked like the witch's house in Hansel and Gretel, tucked away in its hollow, with its pointed gables—were built for John Frederick's grandfather about 1761, by one Captain Robert Smith,. who had fought at Minden under Lord George Sackville, of disastrous notoriety, and who lived for some time at Knole, a parasite upon the house ; they apparently purport to be the remains of some vast house, in defiance of the fact that no upper storey or roof of pro-portionate dimensions could ever possibly have rested upon the flimsy structure of flint and rubble which constitute the ruins. They, together with the Bird House, form an amusing group of the whims and vanities of two different ages. But, to go back to the park, I conclude with the following letter, which is among the papers at Knole :

To his Grace the DUKE *of* DORSET.

My Lord,

    I Elizabeth Hills sister and executor of Mrs Anne Hills deceased of Under River in the Parish of Seal and whose corpse is to be interred in the Parish Church of Seal : but the High Road leading thereto by Godden Green being very bad and unsafe for carriages :" I beg leave of yr Grace to permit the proper attendants to pass with the corpse, in a hearse with the coaches in attendance through Knole Park : entering the same at Faulke [*sic*] Common Gate and going out at the gate at Lock's Bottom : and you'll oblige

Your Grace's most obedient serv^t

UNDER RIVER,   ELIZA HILLS.
18 *Oct.*, 1781.

§ iii

    So much, then, for the setting; but it is no mere empty scene. The house, with its exits and entrances, its properties of furniture and necessities, its dressing-tables, its warming-pans, and its tiny silver eye-bath still standing between the hair-brushes—the house demands its population. Whose were the hands that have, by the constant light running of their fingers, polished the paint from the banisters? Whose were the feet that have worn down the flags of the hall and the stone passages ? What child rode upon the ungainly rocking-horse? What young men exercised their muscles on the ropes of the great dumb-bell? Who were the men and women that, after a day's riding or stitching, lay awake in the deep beds, idly watching between the curtains the play of the firelight, and the little round yellow discs cast upon walls and ceiling through the perforations of the tin canisters standing on the floor, containing the rush-lights ?

    Thus the house wakes into a whispering life, and we resurrect the Sackvilles.

CHAPTER III

Knole in the Reign of Queen Elizabeth

THOMAS SACKVILLE
1st
Earl *of* Dorset

§ i

SUCH interest as the Sackvilles have lies, I think, in their being so representative. From generation to generation they might stand, fully equipped, as portraits from English history. Unless they are to be considered in this light they lose their purport ; they merely share, as Byron wrote to one of their number :

> . . . . with titled crowds the common lot,
> In life just gazed at, in the grave forgot . . .
> The mouldering 'scutcheon, or the herald's roll,
> That well-emblazoned but neglected scroll,
> Where lords, unhonoured, in the tomb may find
> One spot, to leave a worthless name behind :
> There sleep, unnoticed as the gloomy vaults
> That veil their dust, their follies, and their faults :
> A race with old armorial lists o'erspread
> In records destined never to be read.

But let them stand each as the prototype of his age, and at the same time as a link to carry on, not only the tradition but also the heredity of his race, and they immediately acquire a significance, a unity. You have first the grave Elizabethan, with the long, rather melancholy face, emerging from the oval frame above the black clothes and the white wand of office ; you perceive all his severe integrity; you understand the intimidating austerity of the contribution he made to

A CONFERENCE OF ENGLISH AND SPANISH PLENIPOTENTIARIES
AT SOMERSET HOUSE IN 1604

Thomas Sackville, 1st Earl of Dorset, sits at the top right-hand corner, nearest the window.

THE GREAT STAIRCASE

Derek Ad...

English letters. Undoubtedly a fine old man. You come down to his grandson : he is the Cavalier by Vandyck hanging in the hall, hand on hip, his flame-coloured doublet slashed across by the blue of the Garter ; this is the man who raised a troop of horse off his own estates and vowed never to cross the threshold of his house into an England governed by the murderers of the King. You have next the florid, magnificent Charles, the fruit of the Restoration, poet, and patron of poets, prodigal, jovial, and licentious ; you have him full-length, by Sir Godfrey Kneller, in his Garter robes and his enormous wig, his foot and fine calf well thrust forward ; you have him less pompous and more intimate, wrapped in a dressing-gown of figured silk, the wig replaced by an Hogarthian turban ; but it is still the same coarse face, with the heavy jowl and the twinkling eyes, the crony of Rochester and Sedley, the patron and host of Pope and Dryden, Prior and Killigrew. You come down to the eighteenth century. You have on Gainsborough's canvas the beautiful, sensitive face of the gay and fickle duke, spoilt, feared, and propitiated by the women of London and Paris, the reputed lover of Marie Antoinette. You have his son, too fair and pretty a boy, the friend of Byron, killed in the hunting-field at the age of twenty-one, the last direct male of a race too prodigal, too amorous, too weak, too indolent, and too melancholy.

§ ii

The Sackvilles are supposed to have gone into Normandy in the ninth century with Rollo the Dane, and to have settled in the neighbourhood of Dieppe, in a small town called Salcavilla, from which, obviously, they derived their name. Much as I relish the suggestion of this Norse origin, I am bound to add that the first of whom there is any authentic record is Herbrand de Sackville, contemporary with William the Conqueror, whom he accompanied to England. Descending from him is a long monotonous list of Sir Jordans, Sir Andrews, Sir Edwards, Sir Richards, carrying us through the Crusades, the French wars, and the wars of the Roses, but none of whom has the slightest interest until we get to Sir Richard Sackville, temp. Henry VIII–Elizabeth—from his wealth called Sackfill or Fillsack, though not, it appears, " either griping or penurious," a man of some note, and thus qualified by Roger Ascham: " That worthy gentleman, that earnest favourer and furtherer of God's true religion ; that faithful servitor to his prince and country ; a lover of learning and all learned men ; wise in all doings ; courteous to all persons, showing spite to none, doing good to many; and, as I well found, to me so fast a friend as I never lost the like before"; and in this same connection I may quote further from Ascham's preface to *The Scholemaster*, in which he records a conversation which took place in 1593 between himself and Sir Richard Sackville, when dining with Sir William Cecil : Sir Richard, after complaining of his own education by a bad schoolmaster, said, " But seeing it is but in vain to lament things past, and also wisdom to look to things to come, surely, God willing (if God lend me life), I will make this my mishap some occasion of good hap to little Robert Sackville, my son's son ; for whose bringing up I would gladly, if so please you, use specially your good advice." . . . "I wish also," says Ascham, "with all my heart, that young Mr. Robert Sackville may

take that fruit of this labour that his worthy grandfather purposed he should have done. And if any other
do take profit or pleasure hereby, they have cause to
thank Mr. Robert Sackville, for whom specially this
my Scholemaster was provided."

This Sir Richard was the founder of the family
fortune, which was to be increased by his son and
squandered after that by nearly all his descendants in
succession. It was he who bought, in 1564, for the sum
of £641 5s. 10½d., "the whole of the land lying
between Bridewell and Water Lane from Fleet Street
to the Thames." This property, now of course of
almost fabulous value, included the house then known
as Salisbury House, having belonged to the see of
Salisbury, which presently became Dorset House in
1603, and presently again was divided into Great
Dorset House and Little Dorset House, as the London
house of the Sackvilles. A wall enclosed house and
gardens from the existing line of Salisbury Court
south to the river, and shops and tenements in and near
Fleet Street from St. Bride's to Water Lane (Whitefriars
Street). These were not the only London possessions
of the Sackvilles. Later on they overflowed into the
Strand, and another Dorset House sprang up, on the
site of the present Treasury in Whitehall, to take the place
of the older house in Salisbury Court, which had been
destroyed in the Great Fire. It is idle and exasperating
to speculate on the modern value of these City estates.

Sir Richard Sackville died in 1566, when his son
Thomas was already thirty years of age. Very little is
known about Thomas' early life ; we only know that
he went for a short time to Oxford (Hertford), and
subsequently to the Inner Temple. While at Oxford
he attracted some attention as a poet and writer of

sonnets, but I have only been able to find one of these early sonnets, written for Hoby's translation of the *Courtier of Count Baldessar Castilio* (published in 1561), and which I quote, not so much for its worth as for its interest as a little-known work from the pen of one who, as the author of our earliest tragedy, has a certain renown :

> These royal Kings, that rear up to the sky
> Their palace tops, and deck them all with gold :
> With rare and curious works they feed the eye,
> And show what riches here great princes hold.
> A rarer work, and richer far in worth,
> Castilio's hand presenteth here to thee:
> No proud nor golden court doth he set forth
> But what in court a courtier ought to be.
> The prince he raiseth huge and mighty walls,
> Castilio frames a wight of noble fame :
> The King with gorgeous tissue clads his halls,
> The court with golden virtue decks the same
> Whose passing skill, lo, Hoby's pen displays
> To Britain folk a work of worthy praise.

But for the rest concerning these early poems one must take his contemporary Jasper Heywood's eulogy on trust:

> There Sackville's sonnets sweetly sauced
> And featly finèd be.

It seems that Sackville's works were all written in the first half of his life, and that later on, as honours came to him, he altogether abandoned what might have been a first-rate literary career for a second-rate political one—more's the pity. " A born poet " says Mr. Gosse, " diverted from poetry by the pursuits of statesmanship." He is a very good instance of the disadvantage of fine birth to a poet. But for the fact that he was born the Queen's cousin, through the

Boleyns, and the son of a father holding various distinguished offices, he might never have entered a political arena where he was destined to have as competitors such statesmen as Burleigh, and such favourites as Leicester and Essex. Amongst his contemporary poets, Surrey and Wyatt both died while Sackville was still a child ; when Spenser was born, Sackville was already sixteen ; when Sidney was born, he was eighteen ; when Shakespeare was born, he was a full-grown man of twenty-eight. He had thus the good fortune to be born at a time when English poets of much standing were rare, an opportunity of which he might have taken greater advantage had not the accident of his birth persuaded him to abandon poetry for more serious things as the dilettantism of his youth. For he was comparatively young when he wrote both *Gorboduc* and the *Induction* to the *Mirror for Magistrates*. *Gorboduc* was first performed by the gentlemen of the Inner Temple before the Queen in 1561, when Sackville was twenty-five, and the *Induction* was first published in 1563, when he was twenty-seven ; but already in or about 1557, when he was only just over twenty, he had composed the plan for the whole of the *Mirror for Magistrates*, intending to write it himself, although subsequently from want of leis.ire he left the composition of all but the induction or introduction, and the *Complaint of Henry, Duke of Buckingham*, to others.

By the age of twenty-one, however, responsibilities were already upon him. He was married ; and he was a member of Parliament, not merely once but twice over, as appears from the journals of the House of Commons: "For that Thomas Sackville, Esq., is returned for the County of Westmoreland, and also for

33

the Borough of East Grinstead in Sussex, and doth personally appear for Westmoreland, it is required by this House that another person be returned for the said borough." How this double election can have come about I cannot explain. It seems to have done him no harm in his parliamentary career ; not only was he returned member for Aylesbury in 1563, but he took an active part in introducing bills, etc. About this time he went to travel in France and Italy, where for some mysterious reason he got himself thrown into prison ; the reason was probably pecuniary, for we are told that he was " of the height of spirit inherent in his house," and lived too magnificently for his means ; so I think the assumption is in favour of his having got temporarily into debt. If, indeed, he shared in any measure the tastes of his descendants, nothing is more likely. Back in England again, the successes of his career rushed upon him. His father was just dead ; he was the head of his family ; he inherited its wealth and estates ; he was at the propitious age of thirty ; he was related to the Queen ; he was marked out to prosper. Within the next thirty years or so he was, successively, knighted and created Lord Buckhurst of Buckhurst, in the county of Sussex ; given the house and lands of Knole by the Queen, that she might have him near her court and councils ; sent to France and the Netherlands as special ambassador from Elizabeth ; made a Knight of the Garter ; Chancellor of Oxford, where he sumptuously entertained the Queen ; made Lord High Treasurer of England in 1599 ; High Steward of England at the trial of Essex, where he sat in state under a canopy and pronounced sentence and an exhortation, says Bacon, " with gravity and solemnity." By this time, I imagine, he had in very truth become the grave and solemn personage one sees in all his portraits—not that his mind, even in early youth, can have been otherwise than grave and solemn if at the age of twenty he had been capable of imagining a vast poem on so dreary and Dantesque a plan as the *Mirror for Magistrates*, devised, says Morley in his *English Literature*, " to moralise those incidents of English history which warn the powerful of the unsteadiness of fortune by showing them, as in a mirror, that ' who reckless rules, right soon may hap to rue.' " Also, from a letter written by Lord Buckhurst to Lord Walsingham, it is clear that he had no sympathy with ostentation, but only with honest worth: "And, Sir, I beseech you send over as few Court captains as may be ; but that they may rather be furnished with captains here [in the Low Countries], such as by their worthiness and long service do merit it, and do further seek to shine in the field with virtue and valiance against the enemy than with gold lace and gay garments in Court at home." In 1586 Lord Buckhurst was one of the forty appointed on the commission for the trial of Mary Stuart, and although his name is not amongst those who proceeded to Fotheringay, nor later in the Star Chamber at Westminster when she was condemned to death, yet he was sent to announce the sentence to death, and received from her in recognition of his tact and gentleness in conveying this news the triptych and carved group of the Procession to Calvary now on the altar in the chapel at Knole.

He was, in fact, absent from none of the councils of the nation, and I have no doubt that he discharged his duties with all seriousness and honesty. Poetry—a frivolous pursuit—had long since been left behind. The poet had become the statesman. Nevertheless there were times when his very integrity was the cause of bringing him into disfavour with the intolerant mistress he served, notably on one occasion when he refused to take the part of Leicester and was indignantly confined to his house for nine or ten months by Royal mandate. And there was another occasion, amusing as showing the extreme simplicity in which even a man like Lord Buckhurst, who had the reputation of lavish living in his own day, conducted his daily life. Buckhurst, then being at the royal palace of Shene, was desired by the Queen to entertain Odet de Coligny, Cardinal of Chatillon, and did so, but with the result made clear in the following letter, of which I give extracts :

To the Right Honourable the Lords of her Majesty's Privy Council be this delivered.

My duty to your Lordships most humbly remembered. Returning yesterday to Shene, I received as from your Lordships how her highness stood greatly displeased with me, for that I had not in better sort entertained the Cardinal.

He goes on to speak of his " great grief " and his " sorrowful heart," especially, he says, " being to her Majesty as I am," and proceeds with the attempt to justify himself for his supposed niggardliness :

I brought them in to every part of the house that I possessed, and showed them all such stuff and furniture as I had. And where they required plate of me, I told them as troth is, that I had no plate at all. Such glass vessel as I had I offered them, which they thought too base ; for napery I could not satisfy their turn, for they desired damask work for a long table, and I had none other but plain linen for a square table. The table whereon I dine myself I offered them, and for that it was a square table they refused it. One only tester and bedstead not occupied I had, and those

I delivered for the Cardinal himself, and when we could not by any means in so short a time procure another bedstead for the bishop, I assigned them the bedstead on which my wife's waiting women did lie, and laid them on the ground. Mine own basin and ewer I lent to the Cardinal and wanted myself. So did I the candlesticks for mine own table, with divers drinking glasses, small cushions, small pots for the kitchen, and sundry other such like trifles, although indeed I had no greater store of them than I presently occupied ; and albeit this be not worthy the writing, yet mistrusting lest the misorder of some others in denying of such like kind of stuff not occupied by themselves, have been percase informed as towards me, I have thought good not to omit it. Long tables, forms, brass for the kitchen, and all such necessaries as could not be furnished by me, we took order to provide in the town ; hangings and beds we received from the yeoman of the wardrobe at Richmond, and when we saw that napery and sheets could nowhere here be had, I sent word thereof to the officers at the Court, by which means we received from my lord of Leicester 2 pair of fine sheets for the Cardinal, and from my lord Chamberlain one pair of fine for the bishop, with 2 other coarser pair, and order beside for 10 pair more from London.

At which time also because I would be sure your Lordships should be ascertained of the simpleness and scarcity of such stuff as I had here, I sent a man of mine to the Court, specially to declare to your Lordships that for plate, damask, napery and fine sheets, I had none at all and for the rest of my stuff neither was it such as with honour might furnish such a personage, nor yet had I any greater store thereof than I presently occupied, and he brought me this answer again from your Lordships that if I had it not I could not lend it. And yet all things being thus provided for, and the diet for his Lordship being also prepared, I sent word thereof to Mr. Kingesmele and thereupon the next day in the morning about nine of the clock the Cardinal came to Shene where I met and received him almost a quarter of a mile from the house, and when I had first brought the Cardinal to his lodging, and after the bishop to his, I thought good there to leave them to their repose. Thus having accommodated his

Lordship as well as might be with so short a warning, I thought myself to have fully performed the meaning of your Lordships' letters unto me, and because I had tidings the day before that a house of mine in the country by sudden chance was burned . . . I took horse and rode the same night towards those places, where I found so much of my house burned as 200 marks will not repair . . .

This is not at all in accordance with his reputation for hospitality:

He kept house for forty and two years in an honourable proportion. For thirty years of these his family consisted of little less, in one place or another, than two hundred persons. But for more than twenty years, besides workmen and other hired, his number at the least hath been two hundred and twenty daily, as appeared upon check-role. A very rare example in this present age of ours, when housekeeping is so decayed.

I think that this reputation, and the enormous sums which he spent upon the enlargement and beautifying of Knole, make all the more remarkable the statements in the foregoing letter: that he had neither napery, plate, nor sheets, and that in order to provide his guest with a basin and ewer he was obliged to do without them himself. It is apparent also from his will that he indulged himself in the luxury of various musicians, " some for the voice and some for the instrument, whom I have found to be honest in their behaviour and skilful in their profession, and who had often given me after the labour and painful travels of the day much recreation and contatation with their delightful harmony." " Musicians," it was said, " the most curious he could have," so that in these extravagances he was not parsimonious, although he disregarded the common comforts of life.

In June 1566 Queen Elizabeth had presented him

with Knole, but, because the house was then both let and sub-let, it was not until 1603 that he was able to take possession. Tradition says that the Queen bestowed Knole upon him because she wished to have him nearer to her court and councils, and to spare him the constant journey between London and Buckhurst, over the rough, clay-sodden roads of the Weald, at that date still an uncultivated and almost uninhabited district, where droves of wild swine rootled for acorns under the oaks. He does not appear to have spent very much time at Knole during the first years of his ownership, for in a letter written in September 1605, to Lord Salisbury, he says : " I go now to Horsley, and thence to Knole, where I was not but once in the first beginnings all the year, whence for three or four days to Buckhurst, where I was not these seven years." This did not prevent him from spending a great deal of money on the house ; unfortunately there is no record of what he spent between 1603 and 1607, but for the last ten months of his life alone there is a total, spent on buildings, material, and stock, for four thousand one hundred and seven pounds, eleven shillings, and ninepence—an equivalent, in round figures, to forty thousand of modern money. To account for these sums, it is known that he built the Great Staircase, transformed the Great Hall to its present state, and put in the plaster-work ceilings and marble chimney-pieces. He also put up the very lovely lead water-spouts in the courtyards.

The good fortune of Lord Buckhurst did not come to an end with the death of Queen Elizabeth. He was one of those who travelled to meet the new King on his journey down from the North, was confirmed by him in his tenure of the office of Lord Treasurer, and early in the following year was created Earl of Dorset. The illuminated patents of creation are at Knole, showing portraits of both Elizabeth and James I, not very flattering to either; and the Lord Treasurer's chest is at Knole likewise, a huge coffer covered in leather and thickly studded with large round-headed brass nails. There is a warrant, signed by him as Lord Treasurer, for increasing the duty on tobacco, "That tobacco, being a drug brought into England of late years in small quantities, was used and taken by the better sort only as physic to preserve health; but through evil custom and the toleration thereof that riotous and disorderly persons spent most of their time in that idle vanity." This warrant, which is dated 1605, shows how little time had elapsed since its introduction before tobacco established its popularity.

He was now advancing in years, and his own letters prove that his health was not very good. In one letter, written to Cecil, he complains that he cannot rest more than two or three hours in the night at most, also that he is constantly subject to rheums and cold and coughs, forced to defend himself with warmth, and to fly the air in cold or moist weathers. In another letter, also written to Cecil, he again complains of a cough, and says that he cannot come abroad for three or four days at least. But his devotion to his public affairs was greater than his attention to his health, for he says, " I have by the space of this month and more foreborne to take physic by reason of her Majesty's business, and now having this only week left for physic I am resolved to prevent sickness, feeling myself altogether distempered and filled with humours, so as if her Majesty should miss me I beseech you in respect hereof to excuse me." In 1607, when the old man was seventy-one, there was a report current in London that he was dead, but on the King sending him a diamond, and wishing that he might live so long as that ring would continue, " My Lord Treasurer," says a letter dated June 1607, " revived again." In the following year, however, he died dramatically in harness, of apoplexy while sitting at the Council table in Whitehall. His funeral service took place in Westminster Abbey, but his body was taken to Withyham, where it now lies buried in the vault of his ancestors.

§ iii

I have dealt as briefly as possible with the Lord Treasurer's life, because no one could pretend that the history of his embassies or his occupations of office could have any interest save to a student of the age of Elizabeth. But as a too-much-neglected poet I should like presently to quote the opinions of those well qualified to judge, showing that he was, at least, something of a pioneer in English literature—crude, of course, and uniformly gloomy ; too gloomy to read, save as a labour of love or conscience ; but nevertheless the author—or part-author—of the earliest English tragedy, and, in some passages, a poet of a certain sombre splendour. That he was a true poet, I think, is unquestionable, unlike his descendant Charles, who by virtue of one song in particular continues to survive in anthologies, but who was probably driven into verse by the fashion of his age rather than by any genuine urgency of creation.

The tragedy of *Gorboduc*, whose title was afterwards altered to *Ferrex and Porrex*, was written in collaboration with Thomas Norton, although the exact share of each author is not precisely known and has been much argued.

To the modern reader [says Professor Saintsbury] *Gorboduc* is scarcely inviting, but that is not a condition of its attractiveness to its own contemporaries. [It] is of the most painful regularity ; and the scrupulosity with which each of the rival princes is provided with a counsellor and a parasite to himself, and the other parts are allotted with similar fairness, reaches such a point that it is rather surprising that *Gorboduc* was not provided with two queens—a good and a bad. But even these faults are perhaps less trying to the modern reader than the inchoate and unpolished condition of the metre in the choruses, and indeed in the blank verse dialogue. Here and there there are signs of the stateliness and poetical imagery of the *Induction*, but for the most part the decasyllables stop dead at their close and begin afresh at their beginning with a staccato movement and a dull monotony of cadence which is inexpressibly tedious.

Professor Saintsbury rightly points out that the dullness of *Gorboduc* to our ideas is not a criterion of the effect it produced on readers of its own day. Sir Philip Sidney, for example, while excepting it from the particular charges he brings against all other English tragedies and comedies, and granting that " it is full of stately speeches and well-sounding phrases, climbing to the height of Seneca his style, and as full of notable morality, which it doth most delightfully teach, and so obtain the very end of poesy," finds fault with it in an unexpected quarter, namely, that it fails in two unities, of time and place, so that the modern criticism of its " painful regularity " was far from occurring to a mind intent upon a yet more rigorous form.

In spite of its manifest imperfections [says the Cambridge Modern History], the tragedy of *Gorboduc* has two supreme claims to honourable commemoration. It introduced Englishmen who knew no language but their own to an artistic conception of tragedy, and it revealed to them the true mode of tragic expression.

I might also quote here the sonnet of a greater poet, who owed much, if not to *Gorboduc*, at least to the *Induction*—Edmund Spenser.

> *In vain I think, right honourable lord,*
> *By this rude rhyme to memorize thy name,*
> *Whose learnèd muse hath writ her own record*
> *In golden verse worthy immortal fame.*
> *Thou much more fit (were leisure to the same)*
> *Thy gracious sovereign's praises to compile,*
> *And her imperial majesty to frame*
> *In lofty numbers and heroic style.*
> *But sith thou may'st not so, give leave awhile*
> *To baser wit his power therein to spend,*
> *Whose gross defaults thy dainty pen may file,*
> *And unadvisèd oversights amend.*
> *But evermore vouchsafe it to maintain*
> *Against vile Zoylus' backbitings vain.*

There is also a sonnet by Joshua Sylvester, of which I will only quote the anagram prefixed to it :

Sackvilus   Comes Dorsetius
Vas Lucis   *Esto decor Musis*
    Sacris Musis celo devotus

But although there can scarcely be two opinions about *Gorboduc*—that it is sometimes noble, and always dull—Sackville's two other poems, the *Induction* to the *Mirror for Magistrates* and the *Complaint of Henry Duke of Buckingham*, have never met with the recognition they deserve, save for the discriminating applause of men of letters. I do not say that they are works which can be read through with an unvarying degree of pleasure ; there are stagnant passages which have to be waded through in between the more

43

admirable portions. But such portions, when they are reached, do contain much of the genuine stuff of poetry, impressive imagery, a surprising absence of cumbersome expression—especially when the reader bears in mind that Sackville was writing before Spenser, and long before Marlowe—and a diction which is consistently dignified and suitable to the gravity of the theme. Take these stanzas for instance :

> *And first within the porch and jaws of hell*
> *Sat deep* Remorse of Conscience, *all besprent*
> *With tears ; and to herself oft would she tell*
> *Her wretchedness, and cursing never stent*
> *To sob and sigh ; but ever thus lament,*
> > *With thoughtful care, as she that, all in vain,*
> > *Would wear and waste continually in pain.*

> *Next saw we* Dread, *all trembling : how he shook*
> *With foot uncertain, proffered here and there,*
> *Benumbed of speech, and, with a ghastly look,*
> *Searched every place, all pale and dead for fear,*
> *His cap borne up with staring of his hair,*
> > *'Stoin'd and amazed at his own shade for dread*
> > *And fearing greater dangers than he need.*

> *And next, in order sad,* Old Age *we found,*
> *His beard all hoar, his eyes hollow and blind,*
> *With drooping cheer still poring on the ground,*
> *As on the place where Nature him assigned*
> *To rest, when that the sisters had untwined*
> > *His vital thread, and ended with their knife*
> > *The fleeting course of fast-declining life.*

These stanzas are from the *Induction.* Or take the following from the *Complaint of the Duke of Buckingham* :

> *Midnight was come, and every vital thing*
> *With sweet sound sleep their weary limbs did rest ;*

THE GREAT STAIRCASE

Country Life

THE STONE COURT

The beasts were still, the little birds that sing
Now sweetly slept beside their mother's breast,
The old and all well shrouded in their nest ;
The waters calm, the cruel seas did cease,
The woods, the fields, and all things held their peace.

The golden stars were whirled amid their race,
And on the earth did with their twinkling light,
When each thing nestled in his resting place,
Forget day's pain with pleasure of the night ;
The fearful deer of death stood not in doubt,
The partridge dreamt not of the falcon's foot.

These quotations will give some kind of idea of Sackville's matter and manner, and of the *Mirror*, which survives among the classic monuments of English poetry, says Courthope, only by virtue of the genius of Sackville. For the rest, not wishing to be thought prejudiced, I should like to quote copiously from Professor Saintsbury's *Elizabethan Literature*, since therein is expressed, a great deal better than I could express it, my own view of Sackville's poetry, and by calling in the testimony of so excellent, scholarly, and delightful an authority I may be freed from the charge of partiality which I should not at all like to incur.

The next remarkable piece of work done in English poetry after Tottel's *Miscellany*—a piece of work of greater actual poetic merit than anything in the *Miscellany* itself—was . . . the famous *Mirror for Magistrates*, or rather that part of it contributed by Thomas Sackville, Lord Buckhurst . . . The *Induction* and the *Complaint of Buckingham*, which Sackville furnished to it in 1559, though they were not published till four years later, completely outweigh all the rest in value. His contributions to the *Mirror for Magistrates* contain the best poetry written in the English language between Chaucer and Spenser, and are most certainly the originals or at least the models of some of Spenser's finest work. He has had but faint praise of late years . . . I have little hesitation in saying that no more astonishing contribution to English poetry, when the due reservations of that historical criticism which is the life of all criticism are made, is to be found anywhere. The bulk is not great : twelve or fifteen hundred lines must cover the whole of it. The form is not new, being merely the 7-line stanza already familiar in Chaucer. The arrangement is in no way novel, combining as it does the allegorical presentment of embodied virtues, vices, and qualities with the melancholy narrative common in poets for many years before. But the poetical value of the whole is extraordinary. The two constituents of that value, the formal and the material, are represented here with a singular equality of development. There is nothing here of Wyatt's floundering prosody, nothing of the well-intentioned doggerel in which Surrey himself indulges and in which his pupils simply revel. The cadences of the verse perfect, the imagery fresh and sharp, the presentation of nature singularly original, when it is compared with the battered copies of the poets with whom Sackville must have been most familiar, the followers of Chaucer from Occleeve to Hawes. Even the general plan of the poem—the weakest part of nearly all poems of this time—is extraordinarily effective and makes one sincerely sorry that Sackville's taste or his other occupations did not permit him to carry out the whole scheme on his own account. The *Induction*, in which the author is brought face to face with Sorrow, and the central passages of the *Complaint of Buckingham*, have a depth and fullness of poetical sound and sense for which we must look backwards a hundred and fifty years, or forwards nearly five and twenty . . . .

He has not indeed the manifold music of Spenser—it would be unreasonable to expect that he should have it. But his stanzas are of remarkable melody, and they have about them a command, a completeness of accomplishment within the writer's intentions, which is very noteworthy in so young a man. The extraordinary richness and stateliness of the measure has escaped no critic. There is indeed a certain one-sidedness about it, and a devil's advocate might urge that a long poem couched in verse (let alone the subject) of such unbroken gloom would be intolerable. But Sackville did not write a long poem, and his complete command within his limits of the effect at which he evidently aimed is most remarkable.

The second thing to note about the poem is the extraordinary freshness and truth of its imagery. From a young poet we always expect second-hand presentations of nature, and in Sackville's day second-hand presentation of nature had been elevated to the rank of a science. . . . It is perfectly clear that Thomas Sackville had, in the first place, a poetical eye to see, within as well as without, the objects of poetical presentment; in the second place, a poetical vocabulary in which to clothe the results of his seeing; and in the third place, a poetical ear by aid of which to arrange his language in the musical co-ordination necessary to poetry. Wyatt had been notoriously wanting in the last; Surrey had not been very obviously furnished with the first; and all three were not to be possessed by anyone else till Edmund Spenser arose to put Sackville's lessons in practice on a wider scale and with a less monotonous lyre. It is possible that Sackville's claims in drama may have been exaggerated—they have of late years rather been undervalued; but his claims in poetry proper can only be overlooked by those who decline to consider the most important part of poetry. In the subject of even his part of the *Mirror* there is nothing new; there is only a following of Chaucer, and Gower, and Occleeve, and Lydgate, and Hawes, and many others. But in the handling there is one novelty which makes all others of no effect or interest: it is the novelty of a new poetry.

CHAPTER IV

Knole in the Reign of James I

RICHARD SACKVILLE
3rd
Earl *of* Dorset
and
LADY ANNE CLIFFORD

§ i

IT so happens that a remarkably complete record has been left of existence at Knole in the early seventeenth century—an existence compounded of extreme prodigality of living, tedium, and perpetual domestic quarrels. We have a private diary, in which every squabble and reconciliation between Lord and Lady Dorset is chronicled ; every gown she wore ; every wager he won or lost (and he made many) ; every book she read ; every game she played at Knole with the steward or with the neighbours ; every time she wept ; every day she " sat still, thinking the time to be very tedious." We have even a complete list of the servants and their functions, from Mr. Matthew Caldicott, my Lord's favourite, down to John Morockoe, a Blackamoor. It would, out of this quantity of information, be possible to reconstruct a play of singular accuracy.

The author of the diary was a lady of some fame and a great deal of character : Lady Anne Clifford, the daughter and sole heiress of George, Earl of Cumberland, and wife to Richard, Earl of Dorset. Cumberland was himself a picturesque figure. He was Elizabeth's official champion at all jousts and tilting, a nobleman of great splendour, and in addition to this display of truly Elizabethan glitter and parade he had the other facet of Elizabethan *virtù*: the love of adventure, which carried him eleven times to sea, to the Indies and elsewhere, " for the service of Queen Elizabeth," says his daughter in the life she wrote of him, " for the good of England, and of his own person." She gives an account of her own appearance:

I was very happy in my first constitution both in mind and body, both for internal and external endowments, for never was there child more equally resembling both father and mother than myself. The colour of mine eyes were black, like my father, and the form and aspect of them was quick and lively, like my mother's; the hair of my head was brown and very thick, and so long that it reached to the calf of my legs when I stood upright, with a peak of hair on my forehead and a dimple in my chin like my father, full cheeks and round face like my mother, and an exquisite shape of body resembling my father.

After this description, more remarkable for exactness perhaps than for modesty, she adds:

But now time and age hath long since ended all these beauties, which are to be compared to the grass of the field (*Isaiah* xl., 6, 7, 8; 1 *Peter* i., 24). For now when I caused these memorables of my self to be written I have passed the 63rd year of my age.

Having put this in by way of a saving clause, she proceeds again complacently:

And though I say it, the perfections of my mind were much above those of my body ; I had a strong and copious memory, a sound judgement, and a discerning spirit, and so much of a strong imagination in me as that many times even my dreams and apprehensions beforehand proved to be true ; so as old Mr. John Denham, a great astronomer, that sometime lived in my father's house, would often say that

I had much in me in nature to show that the sweet influences of the Pleiades and the bands of Orion were powerful both at my conception and my nativity.

She was innocent of unnecessary diffidence. Yet she was not without gratitude :

I must not forget to acknowledge that in my infancy and youth, and a great part of my life, I have escaped many dangers, both by fire and water, by passage in coaches and falls from horses, by burning fevers, and excessive extremity of bleeding many times to the great hazard of my life, all which, and many cunning and wicked devices of my enemies, I have escaped and passed through miraculously, and much the better by the help and prayers of my devout mother, who incessantly begged of God for my safety and preservation (*Jas.* v., 16).

To her mother she seems to have been excessively devoted ; and indeed, in the midst of this stubborn and peremptory character, the most vulnerable spot is her tenderness for her relations ; those of her relations, that is to say, with whom she was not at mortal enmity. The death of Queen Elizabeth, which occurred when Anne Clifford was a girl of thirteen, was a disappointment to her in more ways than one, for " if Queen Elizabeth had lived she intended to prefer me to be of the Privy Chamber, for at that time there was as much hope and expectation of me as of any other young lady whatsoever," and moreover " my Mother and Aunt of Warwick being mourners, I was not allowed to be one, because I was not high enough, which did much trouble me then." She was not even allowed the privilege of watching by the great Queen's body after it had come " by night in a Barge from Richmond to Whitehall, my Mother and a great Company of Ladies attending it, where it continued a great while standing in the Drawing Chamber, where it was watched all night by several Lords and Ladies, my Mother sitting up with it two or three nights, but my Lady would not give me leave to watch, by reason I was held too young." It is to be regretted that the writer, who possessed so vivid and unself-conscious a pen, should have been thus defrauded of setting upon record the scene in which the old Queen, stiff as an effigy, and blazing with the jewels of England, lay for the last time in state, by the light of candles, among the great nobles whom in her lifetime she had bullied and governed, and whom even in death the rigidity of that bejezabelled presence could still overawe.

Although she had not been allowed to see the dead Queen, Lady Anne was taken to see the new King, but did not find the court to her liking :

We all went to Tibbalds to see the King, who used my Mother and Aunt very graciously, but we all saw a great change between the fashion of the Court as it is now and of that in the Queen's time, for we were all lousy by sitting in the chamber of Sir Thomas Erskine.

This unpropitious introduction was the first she had to James I, but it was by no means her last meeting with him, for she relates several later on which might more properly be called encounters.

About two years after Elizabeth's death Lord Cumberland died, " very patiently and willingly of a bloody flux," leaving Anne Clifford his only surviving child and heiress, then being aged about fifteen years. Her father cannot have been much more than a name to her, for although " endowed with many perfections of nature befitting so noble a personage, as an excellent quickness of wit and apprehension, an active and strong body, and an affable disposition and behaviour," he " fell to love a lady of quality," which created a breach between himself and his wife, and " when my Mother and he did meet, their countenance did show the dislike they had one of another, yet he would speak to me in a slight fashion and give me his blessing . . . . My Father used to come to us sometimes at Clerkenwell, but not often, for he had at this time as it were wholly left my Mother, yet the house was kept still at his charge." All this early part of her life, I ought to explain, is related by her in the Lives of her parents and herself, which she compiled in her old age ; and partly from a diary of reminiscences, a transcript of which is at Knole, and which she appears to have written at the same time as the more detailed Diary which she was then (1616–1619) keeping from day to day. She had a happy childhood with her mother, and cousins of her own age—"All this time we were merry at North Hall. My Coz. Frances Bouchier and my Coz. Francis Russell and I did use to walk much in the garden, and were great with one another. I used to wear my Hair-coloured Velvet every day, and learned to sing and play on the Bass-Viol of Jack Jenkins, my Aunt's boy."

The Diary at Knole jumps without any warning or transition from the reminiscences of youth to 1616. It begins with a sad little hint of the weariness that was to follow: "All the time I stayed in the country I was sometimes merry and sometimes sad, as I had news from London." She had then been married for seven years to Richard Sackville, third Earl of Dorset, grandson to Queen Elizabeth's old Treasurer, who was himself anxious for the match, writing to Sir George Moore about "that virtuous young lady, the Lady Anne

Clifford," and soliciting Moore's good offices with Lady Cumberland.

There were, in all, five children of the marriage : three little boys, who all " died young at Knole where they were born," and two little girls, of whom Margaret, born in 1614, figures largely in the Diary and is the only one to concern us, since Isabel was not born till some years after Lady Anne had ceased to keep the Diary. Lady Anne's mother travelled to London from the North in order to be present at the birth of Margaret, the first child; but by a strange mischance the journey was rendered vain, for, having gone "into the Tower of London to see some friends there, where, the gates being shut up by an accident that happened, she was kept there till after her daughter was delivered of her first child, though she had made a journey purposely from Appleby Castle, in Westmoreland, to London." Not only does the Diary contain constant references to this little girl, but Lady Anne's letters to her mother, now at Appleby, are rarely without some comment—

she begins to break out very much upon her head, which I hope will make her very healthful [a curious theory]. She hath yet no teeth come out, but they are most of them swelled in the flesh, so that now and then they make her very froward. I have found your Ladyship's words true about the nurse had for her, for she hath been one of the most unhealthfullest women that I think ever was, and so extremely troubled with the toothache and rheums and swelling in her face as could be, and one night she fell very ill, and was taken like an ague so as she had but little milk left, and so I was enforced to send for the next woman that was by to give my child suck, whom hath continued with her ever since, and I thank God the child agrees so well with her milk as may be, so I mean not to change her any more It is a miracle to me that the child should prosper so well.

She is but a little one, I confess, but a livelier and merrier thing was there never yet seen.

Dorset also was fond of the little girl, for in other letters to her mother Anne says, after apologising for her bad writing, which she terms " scribbling," " my Lord is as fond of her as can be, and calls her his mistress"; and again, "My Lord to her is a very kind, loving, and dear father, and in everything will I commend him, saving only in this business of my land, wherein I think some evil spirit works, for in this he is as violent as possible, so I must either do it next term or else break friendship and love with him"; and Dorset was, on his side, of the same opinion, for in a letter written to her at Knole, which begins " Sweet Heart," and sends messages to the child, he adds to his wife, " whom in all things I love and hold a sober woman, your land only excepted, which transports you beyond yourself, and makes you devoid of all reason." It would appear that but for this unfortunate question of the lands and money they might have lived happily together, affection not lacking, and on Anne's part at any rate good will not lacking either, as witness her constant defence of him, even to her mother :

It is true that they have brought their matters so about that I am in the greatest strait that ever poor creature was, but whatsoever you may think of my Lord, I have found him, do find him, and think I shall find him, the best and most worthy man that ever breathed, therefore, if it be possible, I beseech you, have a better opinion of him, if you know all I do, I am sure you would believe this that I write, but I durst not impart my mind about when I was with you, because I found you so bitter against him, or else I could have told you so many arguments of his goodness and worth that you should have seen it plainly yourself.

They were married when she was nineteen and he was twenty, and two days after their marriage he succeeded to his father's titles and estates : " We have no other news here but of weddings and burials, the Earl of Dorset died on Monday night leaving a heaire [?] widow God wot, and his son seeing him past hope the Saturday before married the Lady Anne Clifford." In spite, however, of all they had to make life pleasant—their youth, their wealth, and the privileges of their position—they spent the succeeding years in making it as unpleasant as they possibly could for one another.

I hardly think that it is necessary or even interesting to go into the legal details of the long dispute over Lord Cumberland's will. The interest of Anne and Richard Dorset is human, not litigious. It may therefore be sufficient to say that by the terms of his will Lord Cumberland bequeathed the vast Clifford estates in Westmoreland to his brother Sir Francis Clifford, with the proviso that they should revert to Anne, his daughter, in the event of the failure of heirs male, a reversion which eventually took place, thirty-eight years after his death. What he does not appear to have realized was that the estates were already entailed upon Lady Anne ; and that he was, by his will, illegally breaking an entail which dated back to the reign of Edward II.

It is easy to judge, from this broad indication, the infinite possibilities for litigation amongst persons contentiously minded. Such persons were not lacking. There was Lady Cumberland, Anne's mother, bent upon safeguarding the rights of her daughter. There was Francis, the new Earl of Cumberland, equally bent upon preserving what had been left to him by will. There was Richard Dorset, whose own fortune was not adequate to his extravagance, and who, having married an heiress, was determined for his own sake that that heiress should not be defrauded of her inheritance, or that, if she was to be defrauded, he at least should receive ample compensation. And finally there was Anne herself, who was more resolved than any of them that she and the North of England should not be parted. Dorset's part, of the four, was the most elaborate and the most discreditable. He would have been willing for his wife to renounce some of her claims in return for the compromise of ready cash. Anne, however, remained single-hearted throughout : she was the legal heiress of the North, and the North she would have ; and in the midst of the otherwise sordid and mercenary dispute, in which Dorset used every means of coercion, she remains fixed in her perfectly definite attitude of obstinacy, unswayed by her husband, his relations, her own relations, their friends, the Archbishop of Canterbury, and the King himself, their remonstrances, their threats, their vindictiveness, and the actual injuries she had to endure over a long stretch of years. In the end she got the better of them all, and the last picture of her left by the " Lives " is that of a triumphant and imperious old lady, retired to the stronghold of her northern castles, where her authority could stand " against sectaries, almost against Parliaments and armies themselves " ; refusing to go to court " unless she might wear blinkers "; moving with feudal, with almost royal, state between her many castles, from Appleby to Pendragon, from Pendragon to Brougham, from Brougham to Brough, from Brough to Skipton ; building brew-houses, wash-houses, bake-houses, kitchens, stables ; sending word to Cromwell that as fast as he should knock her castles about her ears she would surely put them up again ; endowing almshouses ; ruling over her almswomen and her tenants ; receiving, like the patriarchal old despot that she was, the generations of her children, her grandchildren, and her great-grandchildren.

Before she could reach these serene waters, however, she had many storms to weather, and to bear the " crosses and contradictions " which caused her to write " the marble pillars of Knole in Kent and Wilton in Wiltshire were to me oftentimes but the gay arbours of anguish." Richard Sackville in his own day was a byword for extravagance, and was bent on extorting from his wife for the purposes of his own pleasure the utmost resources of her inheritance. His portrait is at Knole, a full-length by Van Somer ; he has a pale, pointed face, dark hair growing in a peak, and small mean eyes, and is dressed entirely in black with enormous silver rosettes on his shoes. There is also the very beautiful miniature of him by Isaac Oliver in the Victoria and Albert Museum, showing the richness of his clothes, his embroidered stockings, and his hand resting upon the extravagantly-plumed helmet on the table beside him.

His life is an empty record of gambling, cock-fighting, tilting ; of balls and masques, women and fine clothes. " Above all they speak of the Earl of Dorset," says a contemporary letter, after describing the lavishness of some of the costumes worn in a Court masque in which he was taking part, " but their extreme cost and riches make us all poor," and Clarendon says of him, " his excess of expenditure, in all the ways to which money could be applied, was| such that he so entirely consumed almost the whole great fortune which descended to him, that when he was forced to leave the title to his younger brother he left, in a manner, nothing to him to support it." The enormous estates which he inherited, the careful accumulation of the old Lord Treasurer, he sold in great part, in order to squander the proceeds upon his amusements; before he had been in possession for three years he had sold the manor of Sevenoaks, and had " conveyed " Knole itself to one Henry Smith (retaining, however, the house at a rent of £100 a year for his own use), and in the course of rather less than ten years he had sold estates, including much of Fleet Street and the Manor of Holborn, to the value of £80,616, or nearly a million of modern money.

In Aubrey's *Bodleian Letters* there is an anecdote concerning him, not devoid of humour :

He [Sir Kenelm Digby] married that celebrated beauty and courtesan, Mrs. Venetia Stanley, whom Richard, Earl of Dorset, kept as his concubine, had children by her, and settled on her an annuity of £500 per annum ; which after Sir Kenelm Digby married her was unpaid by the Earl : Sir Kenelm Digby sued the Earl, after marriage, and recovered it. Venetia Stanley was a most beautiful and desirable creature . . . sanguine and tractable, and of much suavity.

In those days Richard, Earl of Dorset, lived in the greatest splendour of any nobleman of England.

After her marriage she [Venetia Stanley] redeemed her honour by her strict living. Once a year the Earl of Dorset invited her and Sir Kenelm to dinner, where the Earl would behold her with much passion, yet only kiss her hand.

Later on in his life a certain Lady Peneystone appears, who considerably complicated the already difficult relations between Anne and himself.

Anne Clifford herself, in spite of all that she had to endure at his hands, gives a charitable account of him.

This first lord of mine was in his own nature of a just mind, of a sweet disposition, and very valiant in his own person.

He was . . . so great a lover of scholars and soldiers, as that with an excessive bounty towards them, or indeed any of worth that were in distress, he did much to diminish his estate, as also with excessive prodigality in housekeeping, and other noble ways at court, as tilting, masqueing, and the like, Prince Henry being then alive, who was much addicted to these exercises, and of whom he was much beloved.

What his wife says of his being a great lover of scholars is borne out by his friendship with and patronage of Beaumont, Ben Jonson, Fletcher, and Drayton. Nothing else remains to his credit. He is utterly eclipsed—weak, vain, and prodigal—by the interest of that woman of character, his wife, knowing so well to " discourse of all things, from predestination to slea[1] silk," and by the faithful picture that is her Diary.

§ ii

She is living (1616) principally at Knole, sometimes in London, sometimes making an expedition into the North to join her mother, who in all her difficulties was her counsellor and ally. The perpetual topic of the diary is the dispute with her husband :

" My Coz : Russell came to me the same day, and chid me, and told me of all my faults and errors, he made me weep bitterly, then I spoke a prayer of Owens, and came home by water where I took an extreme Cold."

The Archbishop [of Canterbury] my Lord William Howard, my Lord Rous, my Coz : Russell, my brother Sackville, and a great company of men were all in the gallery at Dorset House, where the Archbishop took me aside and talked with me privately one hour and half, and

Slea = unravelled.

persuaded me both by Divine and human means to set my hand to their arguments. But my answer to his Lordship was that I would do nothing until my Lady [her mother] and I had conferred together. Much persuasion was used by him and all the company, sometimes terrifying me and sometimes flattering me.

Next day was a marvellous day to me, for it was generally thought that I must either have sealed the argument or else have parted from my Lord.

She then starts for the North—a hazardous journey —to confer with her mother.

We had two coaches in our company with four horses apiece and about twenty-six horsemen. I came to my lodgings [at Derby] with a heavy heart considering how many things stood between my Lord and I.

We went from the Parsons' House near the Dangerous Moors, being eight miles and afterwards the ways so dangerous the horses were fain to be taken out of the coach to be lifted down the hills. This day Rivers' horse fell from a bridge into the river. We came to Manchester about ten at night.

Dorset was not above subjecting her to petty annoyances and humiliations, for he sends messengers after her with "letters to show it was my Lord's pleasure that the men and horses should come away without me, so after much falling out betwixt my Lady [her mother] and them, all the folks went away, there being a paper drawn to show that they went away by my Lord's direction and contrary to my will.[1] At night I

[1] The original of this curious paper is now at Appleby, dated April 1st, 1616, and runs as follows: "A memoranda that I, Anne, Countess of Dorset, sole daughter and heir to George, late Earl of Cumberland, do take witness of all these gentlemen present, that I both desire and offer myself to go up to London with my men and horses, but they, having received a contrary commandment from my Lord, my husband, will by no means consent nor permit me to go with them. Now my desire is that all the world may know that this stay of mine proceeds only from my husband's command, contrary to my consent or agreement, whereof I have gotten these names underwritten to testify the same."

Geo. P. King

LADY ANNE CLIFFORD, Countess of Dorset, Pembroke and Montgomery

From the portrait at Knole by Daniel Mytens

THE BROWN GALLERY

sent two messengers to my folks to entreat them to stay. For some two nights my mother and I lay together, and had much talk about this business."

In order to get back to London she has to borrow a coach from her mother, from whom she takes a "grievous and heavy parting." Arrived at Knole, " I had a cold welcome from my Lord," and a day or two later he takes his departure for London, sending constant messengers and letters, to know whether she will give way to his demands. " About this time," she sadly writes—it is April, spring at Knole, and she then aged twenty-six—" about this time I used to rise early in the morning and go to the Standing in the garden, and taking my prayer book with me beseech God to be merciful to me and to help me as He always hath done."

Meanwhile Dorset's threats increase in virulence : on the first of May he sends Mr. Rivers to tell her she shall live neither at Knole nor at Bolbrook ; on the second he sends Mr. Legg to tell the servants he will come down once more to see her, which shall be the last time ; and on the third he sends Peter Basket, his gentleman of the horse, with a letter to say " it was his pleasure that the Child should go the next day to London . . . when I considered that it would both make my Lord more angry with me and be worse for the Child I resolved to let her go ; after I had sent for Mr. Legg and talked with him about that and other matters I wept bitterly."

On the fourth " . . . the Child went into the litter to go to London." There is no comment. It must have been a pathetic little departure.

On the ninth she received, besides the news that her mother was dangerously ill, " a letter from my Lord to let me know his determination was the Child should go to live at Horsley, and not come hither any more, so as this was a very grievous and sorrowful day to me." An unusual bitterness escapes from her pen :

All this time my Lord was in London where he had all and infinite great resort coming to him. He went much abroad to Cocking and Bowling Alleys, to plays and horse races, and commended by all the world. I stayed in the country, having many times a sorrowful and heavy heart, and being condemned by most folks because I would not consent to the agreement, so as I may truly say I am like an owl in the desert.

And a few days later :

My Lord came down from London, my Lord lying in Leslie Chamber and I in my own. My Lord and I after supper had some talk, we fell out and parted for that night.

There was worse to come, for at the end of the month her mother died, " which I held as the greatest and most lamentable cross that could have befallen me," and, mixed up with this sorrow, which is evidently genuine, is the fear that she may be definitely dispossessed of the inheritance of her forefathers. She found, however, that she had the disposal of the body, " which was some contentment to my aggrieved soul." Her sorrows begin to lighten. Dorset, probably perceiving his bullying to be worse than useless against a woman of her mettle, tries a different tack : " My Lord assured me how kind and good a husband he would be to me "; they patch up a reconciliation, and she makes over to him certain of her Cumberland estates in default of heirs ; they agree that Mrs. Bathurst, apparently a bone of contention, should " go away from the Child . . . so that my Lord and I were never greater friends than at this time . . . and my

Lord brought me down to the coach side where we had
a loving and kind parting." He even joined her in the
North, and she records how at Appleby Castle she set
up the " green velvet bed where the same night we
went to lie there," and how " in the afternoon I
wrought stitchwork and my Lord sat and read by me."

She gives many particulars of how she spent her days
in the North. I fancy she was a good deal happier there,
and more at home, and consequently more light-
hearted, than at Knole. At the same time she was
anxious to go back to London to rejoin Dorset, but
this for some reason he was not disposed to allow. She
consoled herself with innocuous occupations :

This month I spent in working and reading. Mr.
Dunbell read a great part of the *History of the Netherlands*.
. . . Upon the 1st I rose by times in the morning and went
up to the Pagan Tower to my prayers, and saw the sun rise.
. . . Upon the 4th I sat in the Drawing Chamber all the
day at my work. . . . Upon the 9th I sat at my work and
heard Rivers and Marsh |read Montaigne's *Essays*, which
book they have read almost this fortnight. . . . Upon the
12th I made an end of my cushion of Irish stitch, it being
my chief help to pass away the time at work. . . . Upon the
21st was the first day I put on my black silk grogram gown.
. . . Upon the 20th I spent most of the day in playing at
Tables. All this time since my Lord went away I wore my
black Taffety night-gown[1] and a yellow Taffety waistcoat and
used to rise betimes in the morning and walk upon the leads
and afterwards to hear reading. Upon the 23rd I did string
the pearls and diamonds left me by my mother into a necklace.

At last the summons came, and " upon the 24th
Basket set out from London to Brougham Castle to
fetch me up. I bought of Mr. Cleborn who came to see
me a clock and a save-Guard [=cloak] of cloth laced

---

[1] Night-gown, of course, has not the modern meaning, as at that date
people slept naked.

with black lace to keep me warm on my journey." Dorset sent in the retinue to fetch her, moreover, a cook, a baker, and a Tom Fool.

Her arrival in London was auspicious : Dorset and a company of relatives came out to meet her at Islington, so that there were in all ten or eleven coaches, and when she arrived at Dorset House she found the house " well dressed up against I came," and the Child met her in the gallery. Moreover, " all this time of my being at London I was much sent to and visited by many " (the young heiress, whose matrimonial disputes had raised so much dust at Court, was an object of interest and curiosity), and she made friends : " My Lady Manners came in the morning to dress my head. I had a new black wrought Taffety gown which my Lady St. John's tailor made. She used often to come to me, and I to her, and was very kind one to another." Such troubles as she had were but slight : " I dined above in my chamber and wore my night-gown because I was not very well, which day and yesterday I forgot that it was fish day and ate flesh at both dinners. In the afternoon I played at Glecko [1] with my Lady Gray and lost £27 odd money." So far, so good. She gave a sweet-bag to the Queen for a New Year's gift, and was kissed by the King. She went to see the play of the Mad Lover ; she went to the Tower to see Lord and Lady Somerset, lying there since their arraignment ; she went to the Court to see Lord Villiers created Earl of Buckingham ; she ate a " scrambling supper " and went to see the Masque on Twelfth Night. She betrays with an unsophisticated and rather charming ingenuity her delight in these

[1] *Glecko*, or *Gleck* : a three-handed game played with 44 cards (eight left in stock). The gleck consisted in three of a kind.

things. But the storm scowled at her over the rim of the horizon, and presently it broke. The first entries are like the splash of the first big rain-drops : " We came from London to Knole ; this night my Lord and I had a falling out about the land." Next day she has Mr. Sandy's book about the government of the Turks read aloud to her, but " my Lord sat the most part of the day reading in his closet." Next day his sulks materialized, and he " went up to London upon the sudden, we not knowing it till the afternoon."

Six days later—there are no entries in the diary to record the suspense of these six days—she is sent for to London to see the King, a higher test for her strength of mind, even, than the former persuasions of the Archbishop of Canterbury. Will she capitulate at last ? or will she come out with her flag still flying ? the tongues of London wagged. The interview is best given in her own words :

Upon the 17th when I came up, my Lord told me I must resolve to go to the King next day. Upon the 18th being Saturday, I went presently after dinner to the Queen to the Drawing Chamber where my Lady Derby told the Queen how my business stood, and that I was to go to the King, so she promised me she would do all the good in it she could. When I had stayed but a little while there I was sent for out, my Lord and I going through my Lord Buckingham's chamber, who brought us into the King, being in the Drawing Chamber. He put out all those that were there, and my Lord and I kneeled by his chair side, when he persuaded us both to peace and to put the whole matter wholly into his hands, which my Lord consented to, but I beseeched His Majesty to pardon me *for that I would never part from Westmoreland while I lived upon any condition whatsoever*, sometimes he used fair means and persuasions and sometimes foul means, but I was resolved before, so, as nothing would move me, from the King we went to the Queen's side, and brought my Lady St. John to her lodging and so we went home.

There is a little note at the side of this entry : " The Queen gave me warning not to trust my matters absolutely to the King lest he should deceive me."

The affair was not allowed to rest there. Two days later she was again summoned before the King, and a sour, unedifying spectacle the majesty of James I must have presented, thus confronted with the young obstinacy of the heiress of Westmoreland :

I was sent for up to the King into his Drawing Chamber, where the door was locked and nobody suffered to stay here but my Lord and I, my Uncle Cumberland, my Coz : Clifford, my Lords Arundel, Pembroke and Montgomery, Sir John Digby. For lawyers there were my Lord Chief Justice Montague, and Hobart Yelverton the King's Solicitor, Sir Randal Crewe that was to speak for my Lord and I. The King asked us all if we would submit to his judgement in this case, my uncle Cumberland, my Coz : Clifford, and my Lord answered they would, but I would never agree to it without Westmoreland, at which the King grew in a great chaff. My Lord of Pembroke and the King's solicitor speaking much against me, at last when they saw there was no remedy, my Lord, fearing the King would do me some public disgrace, desired Sir John Digby would open the door, who went out with me and persuaded me much to yield to the King. Presently after my Lord came from the King, when it was resolved that if I would not come to an agreement there should be an agreement made without me.

After these encounters she retired to Knole, while Dorset remained in London, " being in extraordinary grace and favour with the King." She, poor thing, resumed at Knole the pitiful monotony of her country existence, which to a mind so vigorous must have been irksome in the extreme, and the Diary becomes again the record of her small occupations threaded with the worry and sorrow of her dissensions with her husband. It is illuminating that she never criticizes him ; there are references to his " worth and nobleness of disposition "; her spirit, although high and emancipated enough to stand out against the King in the defence of Westmoreland, could not conceive revolt against the subjection of matrimony. It is an idea which never once enters her head. She even writes him a letter to give him " humble thanks for his noble usage toward me in London " ; but a very little while after this " Thomas Woodgate came from London and brought a squirrel to the Child, and my Lord wrote me a letter by which I perceived my Lord was clean out with me, and how much my enemies have wrought against me."

Conscientious as she is, she no longer finds enough events to justify a daily entry. Perhaps—who knows ? for my part I strongly suspect it—her fighting spirit preferred even the ordeals and excitements of London to the tedium of Knole. She has very little to tell : only the gowns she wore, the books she read, the games she played with the steward, and the ailments of the Child.

At this time I wore a plain green flannel gown that William Pinn made me and my yellow taffety waistcoat. Rivers used to read to me in Montaigne's *Essays*, and Moll Neville in the *Fairy Queen*. The Child had a bitter fit of her ague again insomuch I was fearful of her that I could hardly sleep all night and I beseeched God Almighty to be merciful and spare her life.

This ague of the Child's is a constant preoccupation. I suppose that it was a kind of convulsion, for which the cure was a " salt powder to put in her beer." On certain days a return of it appears to have been con-

fidently expected, for I find: " upon the 4th should
have been the Child's fit, but she missed it," and two
days later she has " a grudging of her ague." There is
a good deal about the Child—never referred to under
any other designation until she attains her 5th birthday, after which she is promoted to " my Lady
Margaret." The portrait of her which is here reproduced hangs over the fireplace in Lady Betty Germaine's sitting-room ; her ring dangles on a ribbon
round her neck, and her hair is done in an elaborate
manner which defied all my efforts, when I was the
same age, to do my own in the same way.

She was an amusement and a consolation, as well as
a source of anxiety, to her mother. Her garments are
carefully noted :

The 28th was the first time the Child put on a pair of
whalebone bodice. . . . The Child put on her red bays
coat. . . . I cut the Child's strings from off her coats and
made her use togs alone, so as she had two or three falls at
first but had no hurt with them. . . . The Child put on her
first coats that were laced, with lace being of red bays. . . .
I began to dress my head with a roll without a wire. I wrote
not to my Lord because he wrote not to me since he went
away. After supper I went out with the child who rode a
pie-bald nag. The 14th, the Child came to lie with me which
was the first time that ever she lay all night in a bed with
me since she was born ;

and another time she speaks of " the time being very
tedious with me, as having neither comfort nor company, only the Child."

For the rest, she was thrown back upon her own
resources. Dorset came and went, and in between
whiles there are small, vivid pictures of existence at
Knole :

After supper I walked in the garden and gathered cherries,

and talked with Josiah [the French page] who told me he
thought all the men in the house loved me.

And again :

About this time [April 1617] my Lord made the steward
alter most of the rooms in the house and dress them up as
fine as he could and determined to make all his old clothes
in purple stuff for the Gallery and Drawing Chamber.

March 1617. *5th*. Couch puppied in the morning.

8th. I made an end of reading *Exodus*. After supper I
played at Glecko with the steward as I often do after dinner
and supper.

9th. I went abroad in the garden and said my prayers in
the standing.

10th. I was not well at night, so I ate a posset and went to
bed.

11th. The time grew tedious, so as I used to go to bed
about 8 o'clock I did lie a-bed till 8 the next morning.

14th. I made an end of my Irish stitch cushion.

15th. My Lord came down to Buckhurst. This day I put
on my mourning grogram gown and intend to wear it till
my mourning time is out, because I was found fault with for
wearing such ill clothes.

22nd. I began a new Irish stitch cushion.

24th. We made Rosemary cakes.

Two days later Dorset arrived from Buckhurst, and
they walked together in the park and the garden.
" I wrought much within doors and strived to sit as
merry a face as I could upon a discontented heart";
but in spite of this entry they seem to have remained
on fairly friendly terms until Easter.

30th. I spent in walking and sitting in the park, having
my mind more contented than it was before my Lord came
from Buckhurst.

5th April. My Lord went up to my closet and said how
little money I had left contrary to all they had told him,
sometimes I had fair words from him and sometimes foul,

but I took all patiently, and did strive to give him as much content and assurance of my love as I could possibly, yet *I told him I would never part with Westmoreland.* After supper, because my Lord was sullen and not willing to go into the nursery, I had Mary bring the Child to him in my chamber.

7*th*. My Lord lay in my chamber.

13*th*. My Lord supped privately with me in the Drawing Chamber, and had much discourse of the manners of the folks at court.

By the 17*th*, My Lord told me he was resolved never to move me more in these business because he saw how fully I was bent;

but evidently he did not stick to this good resolution, because, on April 20th, Easter-day, "My Lord and I had a great falling-out," and a few days later, "This night my Lord should have lain with me, but he and I fell out about matters."

By the next day, however, they were friends again; they played at Burley Break upon the lawn; and "this night my Lord came to lie in my chamber." The next day, too, was spent in peace, and she "spent the evening in working and going down to my Lord's closet, where I sat and read much in the Turkish history, and Chaucer."

So it goes on. It becomes, perhaps, a little monotonous, save that it is always so human, and so modern. One sympathizes with her in her weaknesses even more than in her defiance; when, for instance, she writes amicable letters to all her relations-in-law, sending them locks of the Child's hair, being "desirous to win the love of my Lord's kindred by all the fair means I could," in reality stealing a march upon Dorset in order to get them on her side. One day she chronicles, "This night I went into a bath," but whether this event was of such rarity as to deserve special mention is not explained. At Whitsuntide they all went to church, but " my eyes were so blubbered with weeping that I could scarce look up," and in the afternoon of the same day they again " fell out." But she consoles herself with new clothes—or was that an additional penance ? for she was never given to personal vanity— " I essayed on my sea-water green satin gown and my damask embroidered with gold, both which gowns the tailor which was sent from London made fit for me to wear with open ruffs after the French fashion." Little peace-offerings came from time to time from Dorset; on one occasion he sends " half a buck, with an indifferent kind letter," and on another occasion " My Lord sent Adam to trim the Child's hair, and sent me the dewselts of two deer and wrote me a letter between kindness and unkindness." " Still working and being extremely melancholy " is the entry of one summer day, and a day later, " Still working and sad." A little after this she " rode on horseback to Withyham to see my Lord Treasurer's tomb, and went down into the vault, and came home again [to Knole] weeping the most part of the day." This is perhaps not very surprising. I have been down into that vault myself, and it is not a cheerful expedition. In a small, dark cave underground, beneath the church, among grey veils of cobwebs, the coffins of the Sackvilles are stacked on shelves ; they go back to the fourteenth century, and are of all sizes, from full-grown men down to the tiny ones lapped in lead. But, of course, when Anne Clifford went there there were not so many as there are now ; the pompous ones were not yet in their places, with their rusty coronets, save those of the old Treasurer and his son ; and their blood did not run in the veins of Lady Anne, so on the whole she had less reason to be impressed than I.

The Diary continues in very much the same strain until it comes to an end with December 1619, the year 1618 being entirely missed out. By that time both Dorset and Anne were in bad health; but whereas he was to die five years later, at the age of thirty-five, she, made of tougher stuff, was to survive him by fifty-two years. His last letter to her, written to her on the very day of his death, shows all the affection which was so undermined by that question of her lands :

26th March, 1624.

Sweet Heart,

I thank you for your letter. I had resolved to come down to Knole, and to have received the Blessed Sacrament, but God hath prevented it with sickness, for on Wednesday night I fell into a fit of casting, which held me long, then last night I had a fit of fever. I have for my physician Dr. Baskerville and Dr. Fox. I thank God I am now at good ease, having rested well this morning. I would not have you trouble yourself till I have occasion to send for you. You shall in the meantime hear daily from me. So, with my love to you, and God's blessing and mine to both my children, I commend you to God's protection.

Your assured loving husband
RICHARD DORSET.

"His debts," says one Chamberlain, writing to Sir Dudley Carleton, "are £60,000, so that he does not leave much." In his will he bequeaths to his "dearly beloved wife all her wearing apparel and such rings and jewels as were hers on her marriage, and the rock ruby ring which I have given her," also "my carriage made by Mefflyn, lined with green cloth and laced with green and black silk lace, and my six bay coach geldings."

§ iii

Her portraits change as her years advance, and the lines of determination harden about her mouth. Her true life—the life for which she was most truly fitted— only began after she had passed her fiftieth year, when with the death of her kinsman Lord Cumberland the northern estates passed calmly and naturally into her hands at last. All the quarrels and litigation and anxiety of her youth were left behind her ; she had buried Lord Dorset; she had buried Lord Pembroke after a second marriage as disastrous and as contentious as the first ; she had borne Sackville children and Herbert children ; she had been long-suffering though adamant, submissive though immovable ; she had moped in the sumptuous prisons that were Knole and Wilton ; now she was free to turn tyrant herself over her own undisputed realm. She wasted nothing of the opportunity. Away from London, away from the influence of the Court, entrenched in her numerous castles in the North, she ruled autocratically over her servants, her tenants, her neighbours, and the generations and ramifications of her family. No detail of comings and goings, no penny of expenditure escaped her vigilant eye or her recording pen ; and her diary, that document of intimacy, autocracy, piety, and exactitude, carries its entries down to the very day before her death. With public or political events she scarcely ever concerned herself, but on the other hand no detail of her own private life or of the existence of those around her was too small to excite her comment. Whether her laundry-maids went to church, whether she pared her finger and toe nails, whether her dog puppied, whether she received letters, whether she washed her feet and legs (this is on the 22nd of February, the last occasion being on the 13th of December preceding), whether she kissed the sempstress—all is noted with the same precision and gravity. No anniversary or coincidence is allowed to pass unobserved. That amazing memory extended back over threescore years ; and, moreover, she had the immense volumes of her notebooks for reference, date for date. Her past was ever present to her, the agreeable and the disagreeable merged into one landscape of consonant tone, and whether she observes that this day sixty years ago she travelled with her blessèd mother, or fell out with Dorset, it is with the same complacency and satisfaction at having the tiny anniversary to record. This vigorous mind was not, perhaps, planned on a very broad scale. It was self-centred and self-sufficient ; severe but not reckless ; no fine carelessness endears her to us, or surprises ; even her acts of generosity, and they were numerous, are recorded with the same scrupulous accuracy. She could not give two shillings to a child without setting it down. Her generosity, like all her other acts, was methodical ; she rewarded her servants for definite services with extra wages ; she kept ready to hand a supply of little presents, because it was contrary to her ideas of hospitality that any visitor, however humble, should go away empty-handed, and was careful to consider what particular gift would be most acceptable to the recipient, frequently choosing something of practical utility, such as gloves or lengths of cloth for women, money or ruffles for men ; and these idiosyncrasies run true all through her character, for, conversely, although she was prepared to be generous in her treatment of others, she was equally determined that she

herself should be fairly treated by them, and frequent
are the entries in her diary to this effect : " In the
morning did I see Mr. Robert Willison of Penrith paid
for a rundlet of sack, but I was very angry with him
because I thought it too dear, and told him I would
have no more of him, and then he slipped away from
me in a good hurry." She would always pay cash too,
and bullied her special almswomen, whom she would
not allow to ask for credit with the tradesmen of
Appleby.

Her rights were her rights, and she had always had a
great idea of them. One recognizes the spirit that told
the King she "*would never be parted from Westmoreland*," in the old litigant that went unhesitatingly
and repeatedly to law over niceties connected with
small portions of her estates, content to spend large
sums of money in lawyers' fees if only she could
succeed—as she invariably did—in proving her point.
There is one story which illustrates both her tenacity
and her humour—the story of a certain tenant whose
rent included a hen due yearly to the lady of the
manor. This tribute he neglected to hand over. Lady
Anne instantly had the law on him, spent £400 in
enforcing her claim, won her case, received the hen,
invited her defeated opponent to dinner with her, and
caused the bird to be cooked for them both as the
staple dish of the meal.

So the tranquil and crowded years spun themselves
out for her, and she grew to be an old woman and a
contented one, for she had attained at last the existence
and occupations best suited to her. Her life was full :
the things which filled it were small things, perhaps,
but if they satisfied her who should cavil ? Her
journeyings alone occupied much of her time: those

extraordinary progresses from castle to castle, she herself travelling in her horse-litter, her ladies in the coach-and-six, her menservants on horseback, her women in other coaches, and a rabble of small fry following, so that the miniature army which accompanied her amounted sometimes to as many as three hundred. Often this retinue would include members of her family, or some of her neighbours ; they travelled over the moors of the North, by rough roads, " uncouth and untrodden, those mountainous and almost impassable ways," stopping on the way in those highland villages which had not yet been honoured by a visit from the great old lady or received her bounty, and, coming at the end of the journey to Brougham, to Brough, to Barden, to Skipton, to Pendragon, or to Appleby, Lady Anne would receive her dependants one by one in her own chamber, give her hand to the men, kiss the women, and dismiss them again to their own homes. Her health was no longer very good, but that was never allowed to deter her from her plans : her courage and vigour triumphed always over the treacherous flesh, greatly to the concern of those about her. On one occasion, travelling from Appleby to Brougham, she was delayed at the start by a " swounding fit," when she had to be carried to a bed and laid there near a " great fire " ; much persuasion was used that she " would not travel on so sharp and cold a day, but she, having before fixed on that day, and so much company being come purposely to wait on her, she would go." As she reached her litter, however, she fainted again, " Yet as soon as that fit was over she went." Arrived at Brougham she fainted for the third time, but on being upbraided by her friends and servants for her stubbornness in making the journey,

THE GREAT HALL

EDWARD SACKVILLE, 4th Earl of Dorset, 1589–1652
From the portrait at Knole by Sir Anthony Van Dyck

she replied that she knew she must die, and it was the same thing to her to die on the way as in her house, in her litter or in her bed, and furthermore would not acknowledge any necessity why she should live, but saw every necessity for keeping to her resolution. " If she will, she will, you may depend on't," they said of her, " if she won't, she won't, and there's an end on't."

Now that there was no one to reproach her, as Dorset had been accustomed to reproach her, for her lack of finery and absence of proper vanity, she dressed always in rough black serge, she shaved her head, her fare was of the plainest, and her personal economy was pushed to the length of such small eccentricities as using up every stray scrap of paper for her correspondence. One luxury, indeed, she permitted herself : she smoked a pipe. Into all the details of her household she looked with a careful eye ; already in the days when she was living at Knole she had used up Richard Dorset's old shirts to make clouts , now at Appleby she saw to the preserving of fruit, she had her cheeses made at Brougham, sixteen at a time, she got her coal from her own pits, she had all delinquents into her own room and scolded them till they were probably thankful to be dismissed. At the same time she never forgot those that had served her faithfully ; she would send her own coach to bring some old retainer to visit her ; the marriages, morals, and vicissitudes of her meanest servant were a matter of interest to her ; their marriage portions she made her own affair. Besides her servants, her own family gave her much food for thought and preoccupation : it is true that of her seven children only two—her two Sackville daughters—had lived to grow up, but they by now had produced a cohort of grandchildren, whose visits to Lady Anne were a source of infinite pleasure to the old lady. It is, altogether, a pleasant and seemly end to such a life. She had attained the great age of eighty-six ; her diary was filled with religious references ; she never dwelt upon her death, but it is clear that she can never for one moment have dreaded it. She had lived up consistently to her principles and to her motto : " Preserve your loyalty, defend your rights," and was ready to go whenever the call should come. " I went not out all this day," is the last entry in her diary, and the next day (22nd of March 1676), there is an entry in another hand, " The 22nd day the Countess died."

A Catalogue

of the Household and Family of the Right Honourable RICHARD, EARL OF DORSET, *in the year of our Lord* 1613 ; *and so continued until the year* 1624, *at Knole, in Kent.*

At MY LORD'S TABLE

My Lord	My Lady
My Lady Margaret	My Lady Isabella
Mr. Sackville	Mr. Frost
John Musgrave	Thomas Garret

At THE PARLOUR TABLE

Mrs. Field	Mrs. Willoughby
Mrs. Grimsditch	Mrs. Stewkly
Mrs. Fletcher	Mrs. Wood

Mr. Dupper, *Chaplain*
Mr. Matthew Caldicott, *my Lord's favourite*
Mr. Edward Legge, *Steward*
Mr. Peter Basket, *Gentleman of the Horse*
Mr. Marsh, *Attendant on my Lady*

Mr. Wooldridge
Mr. Cheyney
Mr. Duck, *Page*
Mr. Josiah Cooper, *a Frenchman*, *Page*
Mr. John Belgrave, *Page*
Mr. Billingsley
Mr. Graverner, *Gentleman Usher*
Mr. Marshall, *Auditor*
Mr. Edwards, *Secretary–*
Mr. Drake, *Attendant*

At THE CLERKS' TABLE IN THE HALL

Edward Fulks and John Edwards, *Clerks of the Kitchen*
Edward Care, *Master Cook*
William Smith, *Yeoman of the Buttery*
Henry Keble, *Yeoman of the Pantry*
John Mitchell, *Pastryman*
Thomas Vinson, *Cook*
John Elnor, *Cook*
Ralph Hussie, *Cook*
John Avery, *Usher of the Hall*
Robert Elnor, *Slaughterman*
Benjamin Staples, *Groom of the Great Chamber*
Thomas Petley, *Brewer*
William Turner, *Baker*
Francis Steeling, *Gardener*
Richard Wicking, *Gardener*
Thomas Clements, *Under Brewer*
Samuel Vans, *Caterer*
Edward Small, *Groom of the Wardrobe*
Samuel Southern, *Under Baker*
Lowry, *a French boy*

THE NURSERY

Nurse Carpenter
Jane Sisley

Widow Ben
Dorothy Pickenden

At THE LONG TABLE IN THE HALL

Robert Care, *Attendant on my Lord*
Mr. Gray, *Attendant likewise*
Mr. Roger Cook, *Attendant on my Lady Margaret*
Mr. Adam Bradford, *Barber*
Mr. John Guy, *Groom of my Lord's Bedchamber*
Walter Comestone, *Attendant on my Lady*
Edward Lane, *Scrivener*
Mr. Thomas Poor, *Yeoman of the Wardrobe*
Mr. Thomas Leonard, *Master Huntsman*
Mr. Woodgate, *Yeoman of the Great Chamber*
John Hall, *Falconer*
James Flennel, *Yeoman of the Granary*
Rawlinson, *Armourer*
Moses Shonk, *Coachman*
Anthony Ashly, *Groom of the Great Horse*
Griffin Edwards, *Groom of my Lady's Horse*
Francis Turner, *Groom of the Great Horse*
William Grynes,   ,,   ,,   ,,   ,,
Acton Curvett, *Chief Footman*
James Loveall, *Footman*
Sampson Ashley,   ,,
William Petley,   ,,
Nicholas James,   ,,
Paschal Beard,   ,,
Elias Thomas,   ,,
Henry Spencer, *Farrier*
Edward Goodsall
John Sant, *the Steward's Man*
Ralph Wise, *Groom of the Stables*
Thomas Petley, *Under Farrier*
John Stephens, *the Chaplain's Man*
John Haite, *Groom for the Stranger's Horse*
Thomas Giles, *Groom of the Stables*
Richard Thomas, *Groom of the Hall*
Christopher Wood, *Groom of the Pantry*
George Owen, *Huntsman*
George Vigeon,   ,,
Thomas Grittan, *Groom of the Buttery*

Solomon, *the Bird-Catcher*
Richard Thornton, *the Coachman's Man*
Richard Pickenden, *Postillion*
William Roberts, *Groom*
The Armourer's Man
Ralph Wise, *his Servant*
John Swift, *the Porter's Man*
John Atkins } *Men to carry wood*
Clement Doory }

THE LAUNDRY-MAIDS' TABLE

Mrs. Judith Simpton
Mrs. Grace Simpton
Penelope Tutty, *the Lady Margaret's Maid*
Anne Mills, *Dairy-Maid*
Prudence Bucher
Anne Howse
Faith Husband
Elinor Thompson
Goodwife Burton
Grace Robinson, *a Blackamoor*
Goodwife Small
William Lewis, *Porter*

KITCHEN AND SCULLERY

Diggory Dyer
Marfidy Snipt
John Watson
Thomas Harman
Thomas Johnson
John Morockoe, *a Blackamoor*

CHAPTER V

Knole in the Reign of Charles I

EDWARD SACKVILLE
4th
Earl *of* Dorset

§ i

THE wreckage of Richard's estates devolved at his death upon his brother Edward, who at that time was travelling in Italy. This Edward Sackville was once to me the embodiment of Cavalier romance. At the age of thirteen I wrote an enormous novel about him and his two sons. He had the advantage of starting with Vandyck's portrait in the hall, the flame-coloured doublet, the blue Garter, the characteristic swaggering attitude, the sword, the love-locks, the key of office painted dangling from his hip and the actual key dangling on a ribbon from the frame of the picture—and then the account of his duel with Lord Bruce, his devotion to Charles I, the plundering raid of Cromwell's soldiers into Knole, the murder of his younger son by the Roundheads, the picture of the two boys throwing dice—all this was a source of rich romance to a youthful imagination nourished on *Cyrano* and *The Three Musketeers*. I used to steal up to the attics to examine the old nail-studded trunks from which the Roundheads had broken off the locks. There they were—the visible evidence of the old paper in the Muniment Room, which said, "They have broken open six trunks; in one of them was money; what is lost of it we know not, in regard the keeper of it is from home." There they were, carelessly stacked: on one of them was stabbed the date in big nails, 1623; and there were others, curved to fit the roof of a barouche; of later date these, but all intimate and palpitating to a very ignorant child to whom the centuries meant Thomas or Richard or Edward Sackville; Holbein, Vandyck or Reynolds; farthingale chairs or love-seats. What were dates when the centuries went by generations? The battered trunks were stacked near the entrance to the hiding-place, which, without the smallest justification save an old candlestick and a rope-ladder found therein, I peopled with the fugitive figures of priests and Royalists. I peeped into the trunks: they contained only a dusty jumble of broken ironwork, some old books, some bits of hairy plaster fallen from the ceiling, some numbers of *Punch* for 1850. Nevertheless, there were the gaping holes where the locks had been prised off the trunks, and the lid forced back upon the hinges by an impatient hand. Down in the Poets' Parlour, where I lunched with my grandfather, taciturn unless he happened to crack one of his little stock-in-trade of jokes, Cromwell's soldiers had held their Court of Sequestration. The Guard Room was empty of arms or armour, save for a few pikes and halberds, because Cromwell's soldiers had taken all the armour away. The past mingled with the present in constant reminder; and out in the summer-house, after luncheon, with the bees blundering among the flowers of the Sunk Garden and the dragon-flies flashing over the pond, I returned to the immense ledger in which I was writing my novel, while Grandpapa retired to his little sitting-room and whittled paper-knives from the lids of cigar-boxes, and thought about—Heaven knows what *he* thought about.

Edward Sackville in the big Vandyck was indeed a handsome, rubicund figure, " beautiful, graceful, and vigorous . . . the vices he had were of the age, which he was not stubborn enough to resist or to condemn." What these vices were I do not know; the records of his life make no allusion to them. It is true that the cause of his duel remains a mystery; Lord Clarendon knew it, but beyond mentioning that it was fought on account of a lady, kept his own counsel. It is true also that his sister-in-law, Lady Anne Clifford, disliked him greatly and spoke of the malice he had always shown towards her; but then amicable relationship with Lady Anne was not easily sustained. On the face of it, his life seems to have been loyal and honourable: he suffered considerably for the sake of the cause he had at heart, and his few speeches and letters are full of reserve and dignity, supported by the facts of his own misfortunes; I do not see what more he could have done to deserve the adjective staunch. To me at thirteen he was very staunch and doughty, and one does not willingly go back on one's first impressions. His wife, too, in the pointed stomacher, and the shoes with huge rosettes, governess to the royal children, voted a public funeral in Westminster Abbey, was another staunch figure: severe, uncompromising, but impeccable.

The duel with Lord Bruce was fought when Edward Sackville was twenty-three years old, at Bergen-op-Zoom in Holland, which so late as 1814 still went by the name of Bruceland. In the Knole Muniment room a paper cover was found upon which was written " The relation of my Lord's duel with the Lord Bruce," and the following are in all probability the papers originally contained therein. The " Worthy sir " to whom the letter is addressed remains anonymous, but was evidently some friend in England:

WORTHY SIR,

AS I am not ignorant, so I ought to be sensible of the false aspersions some authorless tongues have laid upon me in the reports of the unfortunate passage lately happened between the Lord Bruce and myself, which, as they are spread here, so I may justly fear they reign also where you are. There are but two ways to resolve doubts of this nature, by oath and by sword.

The first is due to magistrates, and communicable to friends; the other to such as maliciously slander, and impudently defend their assertions. Your love, not my merit, assures me you hold me your friend; which esteem I am much desirous to retain. Do me, therefore, the right to understand the truth of that; and, in my behalf, inform others, who either are or may be infected with sinister rumours, much prejudicial to that fair opinion I desire to hold amongst all worthy persons; and, on the faith of a gentleman, the relation I shall give is neither more nor less than the bare truth. The enclosed contains the first citation sent me from Paris by a Scottish gentleman, who delivered it me in Derbyshire, at my father-in-law's house. After it follows my then answer, returned him by the same bearer. The next is my accomplishment of my first promise, being a particular assignation of place and weapon, which I sent by a servant of mine, by post, from Rotterdam, as soon as I landed there, the receipt of which, joined with an acknowledgement of my fair carriage to the deceased Lord, is testified by the last, which periods the business till we met at Tergose, in Zealand, it being the place allotted for rendezvous; where he [accompanied with one Mr. Crawford, an English gentleman, for his second, a surgeon, and his man arrived with all the speed he could. And there having rendered himself, I addressed my second, Sir John Heydon, to let him understand that now all following should be done] by consent, as concerning the terms whereon we should fight, as also the place. To our seconds we gave power for their appointments, who agreed that we should go to Antwerp, from thence to Bergen-op-Zoom, where in the midway a village divides the States' territories from the Archduke's; and there was the destined stage, to the end, that, having ended, he that could might presently exempt himself from the justice of the country, by retiring into the dominion not offended. It was further concluded, that in case any should fall or slip, that then the combat should cease; and he, whose ill fortune had so subjected him, was to acknowledge his life to have been in the other's hands. But in case one party's sword should break, because that could only chance by hazard, it was agreed that the other should take no advantage, but either then be made friends, or else, upon even terms, go to it again. Thus these conclusions, being by each of them related to his party, were, by us, both approved and assented to. Accordingly we embarked for Antwerp; and by reason my Lord [as I conceive, because he could not handsomely without danger of discovery] had not paired the sword I sent him to Paris, bringing one of the same length but twice as broad, my second excepted against it, and advised me to match my own, and send him the choice; which I obeyed, it being, you know, the challenger's privilege to elect his weapon. At the delivery of the swords, which was performed by Sir John Heydon, it pleased the Lord Bruce to choose my own; and then, past expectation, he told him that he found himself so far behind-hand, as a little of my blood would not serve his turn; and therefore he was now resolved to have me alone, because he knew [for I will use his own words that so worthy a gentleman, and my friend, could not endure to stand by, and see him do that which he must, to satisfy himself and his honour. Thereunto Sir John Heydon replied, that such intentions were bloody and butcherly, far unfitting so noble a personage, who should desire to bleed for reputation, not for life; withal adding, he thought himself injured, being come thus far, now to be prohibited from executing those honourable offices he came for. The Lord Bruce, for answer, only reiterated his former resolution; the which, not for matter, but for manner, so moved me, as though to my remembrance I had not for a long while eaten more liberally than at dinner; and therefore, unfit for such an action [seeing the surgeons hold a wound upon a full stomach much more dangerous than otherwise], I requested my second to certify him I would presently decide the difference, and should therefore meet him, on horseback, only waited on by our surgeons, they being unarmed. Together we rode [but one before the other some twelve score] about two English miles ; and then Passion, having so weak an enemy to assail as my direction, easily became victor ; and, using his power, made me obedient to his commands. I being very mad with anger the Lord Bruce should thirst after my life with a kind of assuredness, seeing I had come so far and needlessly to give him leave to regain his lost reputation, I bade him alight, which with all willingness he quickly granted ; and there, in a meadow [ankle-deep in the water at least], bidding farewell to our doublets, in our shirts we began to charge each other, having afore commanded our surgeons to withdraw themselves a pretty distance from us ; conjuring them besides, as they respected our favour or their own safeties, not to stir, but suffer us to execute our pleasure ; we being fully resolved [God forgive us] to despatch each other by what means we could. I made a thrust at my enemy, but was short ; and, in drawing back my arm, I received a great wound thereon, which I interpreted as a reward for my short shooting ; but, in revenge, I pressed in to him, though I then missed him also ; and then received a wound in my right pap, which passed level through my body, and almost to my back ; and there we wrestled for the two greatest and dearest prizes we could ever expect, trial for honour and life ; in which struggling, my hand, having but an ordinary glove on it, lost one of her servants, though the meanest, which hung by a skin, and, to sight, yet remaineth as before, and I am put in hope one day to recover the use of it again. But at last breathless, yet keeping our holds, there passed on both sides propositions for quitting each other's sword. But, when Amity was dead, Confidence could not live, and who should quit first was the question, which on neither part either would perform ; and, re-striving again afresh, with a kick and a wrench together I freed my long-captive weapon, which incontinently levying at his throat, being master still of his, I demanded if he would ask his life or yield his sword? Both which, though in that imminent danger, he bravely denied to do. Myself being wounded, and feeling loss of blood, having three conduits running on me, began to make me faint; and he courageously persisting not to accord to either of my propositions, remembrance of his former bloody desire, and feeling of my present estate, I struck at his heart; but, with his avoiding, missed my aim, yet passed through his body, and, drawing back my sword, repassed it through again through another place, when he cried, " Oh, I am slain!" seconding his speech with all the force he had to cast me. But being too weak, after I had defended his assault, I easily became master of him, laying him on his back; when being upon him, I redemanded if he would request his life? But it seems he prized it not at so dear a rate to be beholden for it, bravely replying "He scorned it!" which answer of his was so noble and worthy, as I protest I could not find in my heart to offer him any more violence, only keeping him down, till, at length, his surgeon afar off cried out, "He would immediately die if his wounds were not stopped!" whereupon I asked, "if he desired his surgeon should come?" which he accepted of; and so being drawn away, I never offered to take his sword, accounting it inhumane to rob a dead man, for so I held him to be. This thus ended, I retired to my surgeon, in whose arms, after I had remained awhile for want of blood, I lost my sight, and withal, as I then thought, my life also. But strong water and his diligence quickly recovered me; when I escaped a great danger, for my Lord's surgeon, when nobody dreamt of it, came full at me with his Lord's sword; and had not mine with my sword interposed himself, I had been slain by those base hands, although my Lord Bruce, weltering in his blood, and past all expectation of life, conformable to all his former carriage, which was undoubtedly noble, cried out " Rascal, hold thy hand!" So may I prosper, as I have dealt sincerely with you in this relation, which I pray you, with the enclosed letter, deliver to my Lord Chamberlain. And so, etc.,

Yours,

EDWARD SACKVILLE.

LOVAIN, the 8*th September*, 1613

The citations or letters mentioned above to be enclosed in this account of Mr. Sackville are as follows:

A Monsieur, Monsieur SACKVILLE

I, that am in France, hear how much you attribute to yourself in this time, that I have given the world to ring your praises ; and for me the truest almanach to tell you how much I suffer. If you call to memory when, as I gave you my hand last, I told you I reserved the heart for a truer reconciliation, now be that noble gentleman my love once spoke, and come do him right that would recite the trials you owe your birth and country, where I am confident your honour gives you the same courage to do me right that it did to do me wrong. Be master of your weapons and time ; the place wheresoever I wait on you. By doing this you shall shorten revenge, and clear the idle opinion the world hath of both our worths.   ED. BRUCE.

A Monsieur, Monsieur Baron de KINLOSS

As it shall be far from me to seek a quarrel, so will I also be ready to meet with any that is desirous to make trial of my valour, by so fair a course as you require ; a witness whereof yourself shall be, who, within a month, shall receive a strict account of time, place and weapon, where you shall find me ready disposed to give honourable satisfaction by him that shall conduct you thither. In the meantime be as secret of the appointment as it seems you are desirous of it.   ED. SACKVILLE.

A Monsieur, Monsieur Baron de KINLOSS

I am at Torgose, a town in Zealand, to give what satisfaction your sword can render you, accompanied with a worthy gentleman for my second, in degree a Knight ; and for your coming I will not limit you a peremptory day, but desire you to make a definite and speedy repair, for your own honour and fear of prevention, at which time you shall find me there.   ED. SACKVILLE.

TORGOSE, 10th August, 1613

A Monsieur, Monsieur Sackville

I have received your letter by your man, and acknowledge
you have dealt nobly with me, and I come with all possible
haste to meet you.   E. BRUCE.

§ ii

Between this affair and the date of his succession to
his brother Richard, Edward Sackville was employed
on various missions: he sat in the House of Commons,
he was twice sent as ambassador to Louis XIII, and he
travelled in France and Italy. He was thus, when he
succeeded, an experienced man of thirty-four, and he
pursued, uninterruptedly, the sober path of office, now
Lord Chamberlain, now Lord Privy Seal, now a Commissioner for planting Virginia, always in the confidence of the King, and his name affixed to State
documents of the day in noble company. The dis-
graces and follies of his predecessors and of his
descendants were not his lot, if that murderous duel is
to be excepted. My flaming Cavalier, *flamberge au
vent*, was in reality a sober and consistent gentleman;
loyal, but not impetuous; prejudiced, but not blinded;
devoted, but not afraid to speak his mind in criticism;
and in support of this claim I shall presently quote from
one of his speeches in which he argues against a continuance of the Civil War and pleads for a prompt
reconciliation between the King and his Parliament.
His judgment is acute, and his attitude remarkably
sound and broad-minded. Yet at the same time his
devotion to the King was such, that after Charles'
execution Lord Dorset never passed beyond the
threshold of his own door.

There are a few papers at Knole relating to the years
before the war began, and from them one may gather

some idea of the then manner of life, always remembering that Lord Dorset was much impoverished by the extravagance of his brother. The total income for the year 1628 from Knole and Sevenoaks was £100 18s. 6d.—a fifth part of which was derived from the sale of rabbits. Some details of expenses are given in the account-books, besides those which I have already given in connection with the park in the second chapter:

Money spent on the pale in Knole Park for one year (£8 9s. 6d.) *as follows:*

	£	s.	d.
For filling, cleaning, and making six loads of pale rails, posts, and shores, two men	0	8	0
Setting up panels of pales, blown down by the wind against Riverhill, 10d. day each man	0	5	0
Paid a labourer for spreading the mole hills in the meads and for killing moles	0	4	3

The steward of Sevenoaks was paid ten shillings a year, the bailiff of Sevenoaks £10, the steward of Seal £2 10s., the bailiff of Seal £4.

	£	s.	d.
Four hundred nails for the pales	0	2	0
Paid for setting up pales at mock-beech gate	0	0	8
Paid toward repairing the market cross in Sevenoaks	6	8	4

Portions of the park, such as were not already under cultivation of hops, were leased out to farmers for grazing:

The joistment [1] *of Knole Park, May* 1629.

	£	s.	d.
Of William Bloom for 3 yearlings	1	0	0
Of George Dennis for keeping 20 runts [2]	0	13	4
Of Richard Wicking for his kines' pasture	0	13	0
Of Richard Fletcher for summering 2 colts	0	16	0

[1] Joistment: the feeding of cattle in a common pasture for a stipulated fee.
[2] Runts: young ox or cow.

There were other sources of revenue. Letters patent granted an imposition of 4*s.* per chaldron on all coal exported, to be divided among the Earl of Dorset, the Earl of Holland, and Sir Job Harby:

COAL IMPOSITIONS

	£	s.	d.
6th May, 1634	4312	13	0
Deduction for expenses	507	11	4
Rest to be divided into thirds	3805	1	8

That is to say, Dorset's share would be £1268 7*s.* 8*d.*, or more than £10,000 of modern money.

He obtained also £100 a year by devising to Richard Gunnel and William Blagrave for four and a half years a piece of land at the lower end of Salisbury Court, Fleet Street, 140 feet in length and 42 feet in breadth, on condition that they should at their own expense put up a play-house. What would be the rent of such a piece of land now in Fleet Street? Certainly not £100.

In spite of the fact that he complained constantly of his reduced income, Lord Dorset added considerably to the park. He obtained a long lease of Seal Chart, and " all woods and under-woods of the waste or common of the Manors of Seal and Kemsing, viz., upon Rumshott Common, Riverhill Common, Hubbard Hill Common, and Westwood Common . . . in all at least 500 acres."

More entertaining is the acquisition of an overseas estate—no less than that part of the east coast of America which to-day includes New York, Boston, and Philadelphia. Those little manors in the neighbourhood of Sevenoaks, those 500 acres of common land, dwindle suddenly beside this formidable tenure. " An

The sons of Edward 4th Earl of Dorset
RICHARD, LORD BUCKHURST (*left*), THE HON. EDWARD SACKVILLE (*right*)
From the portrait at Knole by Cornelius Nuie

THE LEICESTER GALLERY

island called Sandy [Hook] " the petition casually begins:

An island called Sandy, lying near the continent of America, in the height of 44 degrees, was lately discovered by one Rose, late master of a ship, who suffered shipwreck, and, finding no inhabitants, took possession. The Earl of Dorset prays a grant of the said island for thirty-one years, and that none may adventure thither but such as petitioner shall license.

A second petition takes one's breath away with its magnificent insolence:

The Earl of Dorset to the King. Certain islands on the south of New England, viz : Long Island, Cole Island, Sandy Point, Hell Gates, Martin's [? Martha's] Vineyard, Elizabeth Islands, Block Island, with other islands near thereunto, were lately discovered by some of your Majesty's subjects and are not yet inhabited by Christians. Prays a grant thereof with like powers of government as have been granted for other plantations in America.

Underneath this is scribbled:

Reference to the Attorney-General to prepare a grant. Whitehall, 20th Dec., 1637.

One would wish to evoke for a brief hour the spectres of those of his Majesty's subjects who found these localities uninhabited by Christians.

Returning to Knole after this seems paltry; yet even there Lord Dorset was conducting his affairs on a proportionately large scale. He said himself that he spent £40,000 after his son's marriage, and one can believe it when one reads a sample of the bill of fare provided for a banquet. At the top is written:

To perfume the room often in the meal with orange flower water upon a hot pan. To have fresh bowls in every corner and flowers tied upon them, and sweet briar, stock, gilly-flowers, pinks, wallflowers and any other sweet flowers in glasses and pots in every window and chimney.

BANQUET *at* KNOLE *3rd July* 1636

1	Rice Pottage	17	Tenches, boiled
2	Barley broth	18	Crabs
3	Buttered pickrell	19	Tench pie
4	Butter and burned eggs	20	Venison pasty of a Doe
5	Boiled teats	21	Swans (2)
6	Roast tongues	22	Herons (3)
7	Bream	23	Cold lamb
8	Perches	24	Custard
9	Chine of Veal roast	25	Venison, boiled
10	Hash of mutton with Anchovies	26	Potatoes, stewed
		27	Gr. salad
11	Gr. Pike	28	Redeeve [*sic*] pie, hot
12	Fish chuits [*sic*]	29	Almond pudding
13	Roast venison, in blood	30	Made dishes
14	Capons (2)	31	Boiled salad
15	Wild ducks (3)	32	Pig, whole
16	Salmon whole, hot	33	Rabbits

Another Menu

1	Jelly of Tench, Jelly of Hartshorn	17	Seagulls (6)
		18	Ham of bacon
2	White Gingerbread	19	Sturgeon
3	Puits [peewits]	20	Lark pie
4	Curlew	21	Lobster pie
5	Ruffes [*sic*]	22	Crayfishes (3 doz.)
6	Fried perches	23	Dried tongues
7	Fried Eels	24	Anchovies
8	Skirret Pie	25	Hartechocks [artichokes]
9	Larks (3 doz.)	26	Peas
10	Plovers (12)	27	Fool
11	Teals (12)	28	Second porridge
12	Fried Pickrell	29	Reddeeve pie [*sic*]
13	Fried tench	30	Cherry tart
14	Salmon soused	31	Laid tart
15	Soused eel	32	Carps (2)
16	Escanechia [*sic*]	33	Polony sasag [*sic*]

There is also a list of " household stuff " dated the year of Lord Dorset's succession.

"A Note

of household stuff sent by SYMONDES to KNOLE
the 28th of July 1624."

Packed up in a fardel, viz. : in ye black bed chamber

IMPRIMIS.   A fustian down bed, bolster and a pair of pillows, a pair of Spanish blankets, 5 curtains of crimson and white taffeta, the valance to it of white satin embroidered with crimson and white silk and a deep fringe suitable ; a test and tester of white satin suitable to the valance. A white rug. All these first packed up in 2 sheets and then packed in a white and black rug and an old blanket.

Packed in another fardel, viz. : next ye chapel chamber

IT : A feather bed and bolster, a pair of down pillows, 2 mattrasses, 5 curtains and valances of yellow cotton trimmed with blue and yellow silk fringes and lace suitable, a tester to it suitable, a cushion case of yellow satin, a pair of blankets to wrap these things in, there is also in the fardel a yellow rug, and a white and black rug.

In ye black bed-chamber

IT : Two bedsteads whereof one of them is gilt, which with the posts, tests, curtains, etc., are in all 11 parcels whereof 4 are matted.

In ye black bed-chamber

IT : Packed up in mats 2 high stools, 2 low stools, and a footstool of cloth of tissue and chair suitable.

Next ye Chaplain's chamber

IT : There goes a yellow satin chair and 3 stools, suitable with their buckram covers to them. All the above written came from Croxall.

IT : Packed in mats my lady's coach of cloth of silver, and 2 low stools that came from Croxall, and a said bag, wherein are 9 cups of crimson damask laid with silver parch-

Next ye Chaplain's chamber ment lace, and 6 gilt cups for my lord's couch bed and canopy, and 8 gilt cups for the bed that came from Croxall.

IT : In a wicker trunk, 2 brass branches for a dozen lights apiece ; and 2 single branches with bosses and bucks heads to them, also a wooden box with screws for the said 2 bedsteads, a dozen of spiggots to draw wine and beer, a bundle of marsh mallow roots, and 2 papers of almonds.

IT : A round wicker basket, wherein are 9 dozen of pewter vessels of 9 sorts or sizes.

IT : 4 back stools of crimson and yellow stuff with silk fringe suitable, covered with yellow baize.

IT : 6 pairs of mats to mat chambers with gt 30 yards apiece.

IT : 2 walnut tree tables to draw out at both ends with their frames of the same.

IT : A round table and its frame.

IT : 2 green broad cloth chairs, covered all over, laced, and set with green silk fringe and a back stool suitable, covered with green buckram.

IT : A box containing 3 dozen of Venice glasses.

IT : A basket wherein are 20 dozen o maple trenchers.

And finally, for I fear lest the detailing of these old papers should grow wearisome, there is a letter which so well illustrates the humour, the coarseness, and the difficulties of life at that time, that I make no apology for including it :

Letter

from ELIZA COPE to her sister the COUNTESS *of* BATH

19th Jan. 1639.   BREWERNE

DEAR SISTER,

I AM glad to hear of your jollity. I could wish myself with you a little while sometimes. I have played at cards 4 or 5 times this Christmas myself, after supper, which makes me think I begin to turn gallant now. Some of my neighbours put a compliment upon me this Christmas, and told me the old Lady Cope would never be dead so long as I was alive, they liked their entertainment so well, when my gilt bowl went round amongst them, which saying pleased me very well, for she was a discreet woman and worthy the imitating. I am as well pleased to see my little man make legs and dance a galliard, as if I had seen the mask at Court. I am glad you got well home for we have had extreme ill weather almost ever since you went, but now I will take the benefit of this frost to go visit some of my neighbours on foot to-morrow about seven miles off, but I will have a coach and 6 horses within a call, against I am weary. You know the old saying, it is good going on foot with a horse in the hand.

Commend my service to your lord, and wishing to hear you were puking a-mornings I bid ye good-night in haste.

Your faithful sister,

ELIZA COPE.

§ iii

On the approach of civil war there could be, of course, no doubt on which side the Earl of Dorset would range himself. He had been for many years closely connected with both the King and Henrietta Maria, and Lady Dorset stood in a yet more intimate relationship to the King and Queen as governess to their children. Since 1630, the date of the birth of Charles II, she had held this position, and from this little anecdote it may be judged that she was not so severe a preceptress as her portrait might lead one to suppose:

Charles II, when a child, was weak in the legs, and ordered to wear steel boots. Their weight so annoyed him that he pined till recreation became labour—an old Rocker took off the steel boots and concealed them : promising the Countess of Dorset, who was Charles' governess, that he would take any blame for the act on himself. Soon afterwards, the King, Charles I, coming into the nursery, and seeing the boy's legs without the boots, angrily demanded who had done it. " It was I, Sir," said the Rocker, " who had the honour some thirty years since to attend on your Highness in your infancy, when you had the same infirmity wherewith now the Prince, your very own son, is troubled—and then the Lady Cary, afterwards Countess of Monmouth, commanded your steel boots to be taken off, who, blessed be God, since have gathered strength and arrived at a good stature.

It is no small tribute to Lady Dorset's integrity that after the outbreak of war she should have been continued in her office by Parliament.

I have in my own possession a receipt signed by her for £125 for salary and expenses, 1641.

War became imminent:

"the citizens grow very tumultous and flock by troops daily to the Parliament . . . they never cease yawling and crying " No Bishops, no Bishops ! " My lord of Dorset is appointed to command the train-bands, but the citizens slight muskets charged with powder. I myself saw the Guard attempt to drive the citizens forth, but the citizens blustered at them and would not stir. I saw and heard my Lord of Dorset entreat them with his hat in his hand and yet the scoundrels would not move."

It is clear from contemporary documents that Lord Dorset was preparing to take an active part. He did, in fact, raise a troop which he equipped at his own expense, and with which he joined the King at York. But the old inventories give a list of residue arms and armour indicating a quantity originally more numerous than would be necessary to equip a small troop; the whole house must have been rifled to produce these weapons, all carefully listed, whether complete or incomplete, serviceable or not serviceable, old-fashioned or up to date. One can read between the lines of the list the anxiety that nothing should be omitted which could possibly be pressed into the service of the King. Among the armour at Knole at this date must have been the fine suit of tilting armour, formerly the property of the old Lord Treasurer, and now in the Wallace Collection, described as " a complete suit of armour . . . richly decorated by bands and bordering, deeply etched and partly gilt with a scroll design . . . the plain surfaces oxidised to a rich russet-brown known in inventories of the period as purple armour." This suit, which is one of the gems of the Wallace Collection, had been made in 1575 by Jacob Topp or Jacobi for Sir Thomas Sackville.

" An Inventory

of such arms as are now remaining in the armoury at Knole belonging to the Rt. Hon. EDWARD EARL of DORSET,

first the horsemen's arms & necessaries belonging to them :"

Cornets for Horses	2
Curasiers arms gilt	2
Curasiers arms plain	31
White tilting armour	3
A baryears Armour gorget and gauntlet wanting	1
Sham front for tilting Run plates for barryers	1

Plated saddles suitable to the gilt arms and furniture rotten	2
Old russet saddles trimmed with red leather and furniture defaulting	12
Old russet and black saddles	12
Black leather saddles with all furniture bits excepted	2
Old French pistols, whereof four have locks the other 9 have none and double moulds to them	13
Swords	14
Horn flasks	49
Whereof an old damask one cornered with velvet and many not serviceable	
Slight arms, back and breast 2 gorgets only to them	13

Arms and other necessaries for foot men

One engraven target	1
Partisan rolled with red velvet and nailed with gilt nails and damasked with gold	1
Partisans Damasked with Silver and the Cat on them [the Cat, *i.e.* the leopard]	4
Corslets with back breast cases and head-pieces	138
Spanish picks and English picks with Spanish heads whereof 4 are broken	151
Comb head pieces	70
Old Spanish morions	50
Halberts	7
Bits	6
Full muskets complete	76
Bastard muskets	56
Muskets imperfect	4
Noulds to the muskets	2
New Rests	64
Old Rests	7
Bandeliers	36
Barrels of match wanting 16 bundles	2

(Signed) DORSET. *Jan.* 1641

It was not very long before the Parliamentarians got wind of this hoard, and in August 1642 three troops of horse under the command of one Cornell Sandys rode into Kent, invaded Knole, took prisoner a Sir John Sackville whom they found in charge there, did a certain amount of rough damage, and carried off the contents of the armoury to London. The proceedings were thus officially reported:

Some SPECIAL & REMARKABLE PASSAGES *from both houses of* PARLIAMENT *since Monday* 15*th of Aug. till Friday the* 19*th* 1642.

Upon Saturday night last, the Lord General having information of a great quantity of Arms of the Earl of Dorset's at his house at Sevenoaks, in Kent, in the custody of Sir John Sackville, which were to be disposed of by him to arm a great number of the malignant party of that County, to go to York to assist his Majesty ; called a Council of War, to consider of the same, and about 12 of the clock at night sent out 3 troops of Horse into Kent to seize upon the said Arms ; which they did accordingly on the Sunday following ; and on the Monday brought the same to London and Sir John Sackville prisoner, there being complete arms for 500 or 600 men.

Despite the outcry of plaintive indignation which went up from Knole, the House of Lords report proves that their conduct towards Lord Dorset over the incident was fair, lenient, and even generous:

That the Arms of the Earl of Dorset which were at Knole House, are brought to Town, to be kept from being made use of against the Parliament,

and therefore this House ordered,

That such as are rich Arms shall not be made use of, but kept safely for the Earl of Dorset ; but such as are fit to be made use of for the service of the Kingdom are to be employed ;

an Inventory to be taken, and money to be given to the Earl of Dorset in satisfaction thereof.

Thus ran the official reports; but Knole, astonished, aggrieved, and outraged, drew up a fuller list of injuries. It was the first time rude voices had ever echoed within those venerable walls or rude hands rummaged among the sacred possessions, the first time that orders had been issued there by another than the master. The Parliament men had entered with arrogance, spoken with authority, gone beyond their warrant, and ransacked wantonly—for from what motive but wantonness could they have taken the plumes from the bed-tester or the cushions from his Lordship's own room? or spoilt the oil in the Painter's Chamber? or, indeed, broken forty locks, unless to overcome such slight resistance in an unnecessarily high-handed manner? No doubt the novelty of the experience turned their heads. Rhetorically they were the representatives of the English Parliament, that sober and tenacious senate, as stubborn now as at Runnymede, but in private life they were men, however insignificant hitherto to Lord Dorset, men who, when he passed with a swagger, murmured dully beneath their reluctant deference. The moment when, cantering up over the crest of the hill, they first saw the grey forbidding walls and drew rein before the massive door, their horses' bits jingling and the restive hoofs pawing at the gravel, must indeed have been an experience. Likewise, to ring their spurs on the paving-stones of the courtyards, to pass from room to room followed by a protesting and impotent steward, to stare at the pictures, to lounge on the velvet chairs, to set out their ink and paper on the solid table of the parlour and to draw up their indictment. It was

August; the rose planted beneath the window of a Stuart King to commemorate his visit was covered with its little white blossoms; the turf was smooth and green; the flowers were bright under the young apple-trees in the orchard; the beeches and chestnuts were deep and heavy with the fullness of summer. The austerity of the Roundheads surely stiffened in the soft summer spaciousness of Knole. The owner was absent: they had only his new portrait to gaze at, with scorn of his brilliant doublet and his curling hair.

All things considered, I think that they showed commendable restraint in their behaviour:

The hurt done at KNOLE HOUSE *the* 14 *Day of August* 1642 *by the* COMPANY OF HORSEMEN *brought by* CORNELL SANDYS:

There are above forty stock locks and plated locks broken, which to make good will cost £10.

There is of gold branches belonging to the couch in the rich gallery as much cut away as will not be made good for £40.

And in my Lord's chamber 12 long cushion-cases embroidered with satin and gold, and the plumes upon the bed-tester, to ye value of £30.

They have broken open six trunks; in one of them was money; what is lost of it we know not, in regard the keeper of it is from home. They have spoiled in the Painter's Chamber his oil, and other wrongs there to the value of £40.

They have broke into Sir John his Granary and have taken of his oats and peas, to the quantity of three or four quarters £4.

The arms they have wholly taken away, there being five waggon-loads of them.

Nor was this the last time that the Parliamentarians came to Knole. Three years after these events Cromwell's commissioners were installed there as the head-quarters of the Court of Sequestration for Kent, and held their sessions in the Poets' Parlour, when the Sackvilles were, for a short time, deprived of the property. On this occasion there is no record of any definite damage to the contents of the house, although a House of Commons notice for January 1645 ordered that " two-thirds of the goods and estates of the Earl of Dorset not exceeding the sum of £500 now at Knole in the county of Kent, and lately discovered there, shall be employed for the use of the garrison at Dover Castle, towards the pay of their arrears."

Among the papers in the Muniment Room I find a letter of a later date from Sir Kenelm Digby to Lord Dorset, referring to some stolen pictures which he has been endeavouring to trace in Paris, and recommending to Lord Dorset a certain M. La Fontaine for " the much pains and running about he hath used," suggesting that he should be rewarded with 20s. and recommended to good customers to sell his " powders and cigeours." I wonder inevitably whether the loss of these pictures had been due to any action of Cromwell or his commissioners ? Sir Kenelm's letter, which is long, rambling, and rather illegible, does not make any mention of the cause or date of the disappearance. Sir Kenelm is himself of greater interest, perhaps, than his letter or the pictures. An intimate friend of Lord Dorset's, the author of several housewifely little treatises, such as *The Closet of Sir Kenelm Digby* and *Choice and Experimental Receipts*, he was incidentally the husband of that Venetia Stanley whose lover Richard Sackville had been. (It has, I may mention, been suggested that Edward Sackville, not Richard, was the lover of Lady Digby; and having regard to what I know of Sir Kenelm's character I should think it not inconsistent, even if this were so, that he should remain on most friendly terms with the former lover of his wife. He had, after all, not scrupled to sue Lord Dorset, whether Richard or Edward, for the continuance after marriage of Lady Digby's pension of £500 a year.) Sir Kenelm's portrait by Vandyck is at Knole in the Poets' Parlour; he is a chubby little man, with a fat outspread hand, and dimples in the place of knuckles. At one period of the Civil War he suffered imprisonment, when Lord Dorset, wishing to beguile his friend's tedium, advised him to read the recently published *Religio Medici* of Sir Thomas Browne: Sir Kenelm took his advice, and was so much impressed as to embody his observations in a long letter to Lord Dorset, which was subsequently printed (1643) by " R. C. for Daniel Frere, to be sold at his shop at the Red Bull in Little Britain." I happen to have the first editions of the *Religio Medici* and the little companion volume of Sir Kenelm's *Observations* : the former is heavily scored or commented by some appreciative reader, and attention is called in the margin to favourite passages by the drawing of a tiny hand with pointing finger, the wrist encircled by a cuff of *point de Venise*. Sir Kenelm esteemed his friend's taste, and the " spirit and smartness " of the author, who set out upon his task so excellently poised with a happy temper. Towards the end of his discourse Sir Kenelm quite loses his sense of proportion in his enthusiasm over Lord Dorset's discernment, and exclaims:

Tu regere imperio populos [Sackville] *memento*,

and concludes by dating his letter " the 22nd [I think I may say the 23rd, for I am sure it is morning, and I think it is day] of December 1642," thus proving that he has sat up all night in prison with Sir Thomas Browne—and who in this generation could with truth make such a boast ?

§ iv

More tragical events than the desecration of his house or the imprisonment of his chubby friend marked for Lord Dorset the progress of the Civil War. His eldest son, Lord Buckhurst, was early taken prisoner at Miles End Green with Lord Middlesex and that same Sir Kenelm Digby, and his younger son, Edward, was also taken prisoner at Kidlington, near Oxford, and murdered in cold blood by a Roundhead soldier shortly after, at Abingdon. I know nothing of this Edward Sackville except that he was knighted at an early age, was reported to be " a good chymist," and was deplored in an obituary poem as being

> . . . . *a lamp that had consumed*
> *Scarce half its oil, yet the whole place perfumed*
> *Wherein he lived, or did in kindness come,*
> *As if composed of precious Balsamum,*

and as being to his friends

> *that lost in losing him,*
> *An eye, a tongue, a hand, or some choice limb.*

The author of this poem, A. Townsend, contributed also to the Knole papers a set of verses on the death of Charles I. " It is a shame," he exclaims,

> *those that can write in verse,*
> *Quite cover not with elegies his hearse,*

and asks:

> *Where are the learned sisters, whose full breast*
> *Was wont to yield such store of milk, unpressed ?*

The King, he says, was

> . . . . *pious, temperate, and grave,*
> *Just, gentle, constant, merciful, and brave.*
> *All this, and more, he was not pleased to be,*
> *Without the woman's virtue, Chastity,*

most unlike Solomon, who was wise, yet

> . . . . *did incline*
> *To worship idols, for a concubine.*

Lord Dorset himself took an active part in the fighting. At Edgehill he recaptured the Royal Standard which had been lost to the enemy, and to his answer during the same battle James II later testified:

The old Earl of Dorset, at Edgehill [*he wrote*], being commanded by the King my father to carry the Prince [Charles II] and myself up a hill out of the battle, refused to do it, and said he would not be thought a coward for ever a King's son in Christendom.

I think also that one of his speeches is worth printing, made at the Council table in reply to one of Lord Bristol's which urged the continuance of the war. It is honest, enlightened, bold, and, considering his personal grievances, very dignified:

THE Earl of Bristol has delivered his opinion ; and, my turn being next to speak, I shall, with the like integrity, give your Lordships an account of my sentiments in this great and important business. I shall not, as young students do in the schools, *argumentandi gratia*, repugn my Lord of Bristol's tenets ; but because my conscience tells me they are not orthodox, nor consonant to the disposition of the Commonwealth, which, languishing with a tedious sickness, must be recovered by gentle and easy medicines in consideration of its weakness rather than by violent vomits, or any other kind of compelling physic. Not that I shall absolutely labour to refute my Lord's opinion, but justly deliver my own, which, being contrary to his, may appear an express contradiction of it, which indeed it is not ; peace, and that a sudden one, being as necessary betwixt his Majesty and his Parliament as light is requisite for the production of the day, or heat to cherish from above all inferior bodies ; this division betwixt his Majesty and his Parliament being as if [by miracle] the sun should be separated from his beams, and divided from his proper essence. I would not, my Lords, be ready to embrace a peace that would be more disadvantageous to us than the present war, which, as the Earl of Bristol says, " would destroy our estates and families." The Parliament declares only against delinquents ; such as they conjecture have miscounselled his Majesty, and be the authors of these tumults in the Commonwealth. But these declarations of theirs, except such crimes can be proved against them, are of no validity. The Parliament will do nothing unjustly, nor condemn the innocent ; and certainly innocent men had not need to fear to appear before any judges whatsoever. And he, who shall for any cause prefer his own private good before the public utility, is but an ill son of the Commonwealth. *For my particular, in these wars I have suffered as much as any ; my house hath been searched, my arms taken thence, and my son-and-heir committed to prison. Yet I shall wave these discourtesies, because I know there was a necessity it should be so ; and as the darling business of the kingdom, the honour and prosperity of the King, study to reconcile all these differences betwixt his Majesty and his Parliament; and so to reconcile them, that they shall no way prejudice his royal prerogative ; of which I believe the Parliament being a loyal defender* [knowing the subject's property depends on it ; for, if sovereigns cannot enjoy their rights, their subjects cannot] will never endeavour to be infringed ; so that, if doubts and jealousies were taken away by a fair treaty between his Majesty and the Parliament, no doubt a means might be devised to rectify these differences—the honour of the King, the estate of us his followers and counsellors, the privileges of Parliament, and property of the subject, be infallibly preserved in safety : and neither the King stoop in this to his

Geo. P. King

CHARLES SACKVILLE, 6th Earl of Dorset, 1630–1705
From the portrait at Knole by Sir Godfrey Kneller

THE VENETIAN AMBASSADOR'S BEDROOM

subjects, nor the subjects be deprived of their just liberties by the King. And whereas my Lord of Bristol observes, " that in Spain very few civil dissensions arise, because the subjects are truly subjects, and the Sovereign truly a Sovereign "; that is, as I understand, the subjects are scarcely removed a degree from slaves, nor the Sovereign from a tyrant ; here in England the subjects have, by long-received liberties granted to our ancestors by their Kings, made their freedom resolve into a second nature ; and neither is it safe for our Kings to strive to introduce the Spanish Government upon these free-born nations, nor just for the people to suffer that Government to be imposed upon them, which I am certain his Majesty's goodness never intended. And whereas my Lord of Bristol intimates the strength and bravery of our army as an inducement to the continuation of these wars, which he promises himself will produce a fair and happy peace ; in this I am utterly repugnant to his opinion ; for, grant that we have an army of gallant and able men, which, indeed, cannot be denied, yet we have infinite disadvantages on our side, the Parliament having double our number, and surely [though our enemies] persons of as much bravery, nay, and sure to be daily supported, when any of their number fails ; a benefit which we cannot bestow, they having the most populous part of the kingdom at their devotion ; all, or most, of the cities, considerable towns and ports, together with the mainest pillar of the kingdom's safety, the sea, at their command, and the navy ; and, which is most material of all, an inexhaustible Indies of money to pay their soldiers, out of the liberal contributions of coin and plate sent in by people of all conditions, who account the Parliament's cause their cause, and so think themselves engaged to part with the uttermost penny of their estates in their defence, whom they esteem the patriots of their liberties. These strengths of theirs and the defects of ours considered, I conclude it necessary for all our safeties, and the good of the whole Commonwealth, to beseech his Majesty to take some present order for a treaty of peace betwixt himself and his high court of Parliament, who, I believe, are so loyal and obedient to his sacred Majesty, that they will propound nothing that shall be prejudicial to his royal prerogative, or repugnant to their fidelity and duty.

It is, of course, not at all to my purpose to follow the course of the Civil War, but only to say that after the execution of the King Lord Dorset made a vow, which he is believed to have kept, that he would never again stir out of his house until he should be carried out of it in his coffin. He did not, in point of fact, survive the King by very many years, but died in 1652 and was buried at Withyham.

CHAPTER VI

Knole in the Reign of Charles II

CHARLES
6th
Earl *of* Dorset

§ i

EDWARD SACKVILLE was succeeded by his son Richard, married to Lady Frances Cranfield, a considerable heiress, who, on the death of her brother, inherited the fortune and property of their father, Lionel Cranfield, Earl of Middlesex, sometime Treasurer to James I. I mention this marriage especially, because it brought to the Sackvilles the house called Copt Hall in Essex and its contents, which included much of the finest furniture now at Knole, some of the tapestry, the many portraits of the Cranfields by Mytens and Dobson, the series of historical portraits in the Brown Gallery, and the Mytens copies of Raphael's cartoons. There are a number of receipts at Knole to no less than six different carriers, for wagon-loads of effects removed from Copt Hall to Knole at the cost of £2. 5s. per load. From Copt Hall also came the carved stone shield now in the Stone Court on the roof of the Great Hall. The Copt Hall estate was sold in 1701 for the approximate sum of twenty thousand pounds. The draft of the marriage settlement is at Knole:

January 25th, 1640

The Earl of Middlesex is to assure ten thousand pounds to the Earl of Dorset in marriage with the Lady Frances

Cranfield to the Lord Buckhurst to be paid in times and manner following :

He is to retain the money in his hands, paying yearly to the young couple towards their maintenance by equal portions at Michaelmas and our Lady Day £800 per annum until a jointure be made of £1500 per annum, by the Lord Buckhurst joining with the Earl of Dorset when he shall come to full age.

And if the Lord Buckhurst [which God forbid] shall decease before the said lady, or a jointure so made, then the ten thousand pound shall be the sole use of the said lady. But if the said lady [which God forbid] should die before the the Lord Buckhurst without children, the said portion or so much shall remain not laid out by consent of the Earl of Dorset in purchasing in lands or leases, shall be paid to the said Earl of Dorset.

And in the same connection there are some notes from Edward, Lord Dorset to Lord Middlesex, one written " this Thursday morning at 5 of the clock," apologising for the " bad character " which Lord Middlesex must decipher—and indeed the writing is all but illegible—but he is obliged to write as he must go presently into Kent to dispose some bargains and sales.

No particular interest attaches to Richard Sackville, save that he translated *Le Cid* into English verse and wrote a poem on Ben Jonson, but there are at Knole some memorandum books in his handwriting (between 1660 and 1670) which are worth quoting, I think, for the following illuminating extracts:

From the DIARY *of* SERVANTS' *faults*

	£	s.	d.
Henry Mattock, for scolding to extremity on Sunday without cause	0	0	3

	£	s.	d.
William Loe, for running out of doors from Morning till Midnight without leave	0	2	0
Richard Meadowes, for being absent when my Lord came home late, and making a headless excuse	0	0	6
Henry Mattock, for not doing what he is bidden	0	1	0

And 3*d.* a day till he does from this day.

	£	s.	d.
Henry Mattock, for disposing of my cast linen without my order	0	0	3
Robert Verrell, for giving away my money	0	0	6
Henry Mattock, for speaking against going to Knole	0	0	6

Verrell to pay for not burning the brakes out of the Wilderness, 3*d.* per week out of his week's wages of 5*s.* for forty-two weeks.

There are various other notes in the same books: Thomas Porter, going to Knole, was to have five shillings a week board-wages; and, judging from the following, Lord Dorset evidently could not wholly trust his memory unaided: " My French shot-bag; an hammer, and some playthings for Tom, a bone knife, etc. A great Iron chafing-dish, or a fire-pan to set it upon." And again, " A silver porringer for little Tom."

Another day he notes:

Old lead cast at Knole for the two turrets weighing 1500 lbs. Old lead cast for the cistern weighing 1200 lbs. Sold 13th Aug. 1662 to Edmund Giles and Edward Bourne the Advowson of the Rectory and Parsonage of Tooting in Surrey for an £100 and paid my wife.

There is also a receipt:

Nov. 14, 1671. Rec^D of the Right Hon. RICHARD Earl of DORSET, in full of all wages bills and accounts whatsoever *from ye beginning of ye World to this day* ye full sum of five pounds seven shillings and sixpence I say rec'd by JOHN WALL GROVE.

§ ii

This Richard Sackville and Frances Cranfield had seven sons and six daughters. There are some delightful portraits of the little girls at Knole, one in particular of Lady Anne and Lady Frances, painted in a garden, leading a squirrel on a blue ribbon, and in the chapel at Withyham there is an elaborate monument to commemorate the youngest son, Thomas, no doubt the " little Tom " for whom the playthings and the silver porringer were to be remembered. The monument bears the following inscription:

Stand not amaz'd [Reader] to see us shed
From drowned eyes vain offerings to ye dead
For he whose sacred ashes here doth lie
Was the great hopes of all our family.
To blaze whose virtues is but to detract
From them, for in them none can be exact.
So grave and hopeful was his youth,
So dear a friend to piety and truth,
He scarce knew sin, but what curst nature gave,
And yet grim death hath snatch'd him to his grave.
He never to his Parents was unkind
But in his early leaving them behind,
And since hath left us and for e'er is gone
What Mother would not weep for such a Son—
May this fair Monument then never fade,
Or be by blasting time or age decay'd.
That the succeeding times to all may tell
Here lieth one that liv'd and died well—
Here lies the thirteenth child and seventh son
Who in his thirteenth year his race had run.
THOMAS SACKVILLE.

Of the other children, save of the eldest, there is no record, or none worth quoting: many of them died, as happened with such pitiable frequency, at a very early age: Lionel, aged three; Catherine, aged one; Cranfield, aged fourteen days; Elizabeth, aged two years; Anne, aged three. The eldest son, however, is one of the most jovial and debonair figures in the Knole portrait-gallery, Charles, the sixth Earl—let us call him the Restoration Earl—the jolly, loose-living, magnificent Mæcenas, " during the whole of his life the patron of men of genius and the dupe of women, and bountiful beyond measure to both." He furnished Knole with silver, and peopled it with poets and courtesans; he left us the Poets' Parlour, rich with memories of Pope and Dryden, Prior and Shadwell, D'Urfey and Killigrew; he left us the silver and ebony stands on which he was in the habit in hours of relaxation of placing his cumbersome periwig; he left us his portraits, both as the bewigged and be-ribboned courtier, and as the host, wrapped in a loose robe, a turban twisted round his head; he left us his gay and artificial stanzas to Chloris and Dorinda, and his rousing little song written on the eve of a naval engagement. He is not, perhaps, a very admirable figure. He was not above trafficking in court appointments; he disturbed London by a rowdy youth; he was reported to have passed on his mistresses to the King; he ended his life in mental and moral decay with a squalid woman at Bath. He followed the fashions of his age, and the most that can be claimed for him is that he should stand, along with his inseparables Rochester and Sedley, as the prototype of that age. But for all that, there is about such geniality, such generosity, and such munificence, a certain coarse lovableness which holds an indestructible charm for the English race. It is that which makes Charles the Second a more popular monarch than William the Third: Herrick a more popular poet than Milton. Last but not least, Charles Sackville is connected with that most attractive figure of the English stage—Nell Gwyn.

It is not known precisely in what year he was born, but it was either 1639, 1640, or 1642, so that he must have been a young man somewhere in the neighbourhood of twenty when Charles II came to the throne. He had been educated by a tutor, one Jennings, and sent abroad with him: as Jennings wrote home of him in measured terms surprising in that age of sycophancy, saying " I doubt not he will attain to some perfection," he probably held but a low opinion of the abilities of his pupil. I do not know at what age Lord Buckhurst, as he then was, returned to England, but he must have been quite young, for in 1660 he becomes Colonel of a regiment of foot, commands 104 men, and receives a yearly allowance of £70 from his father, and the references to him in Pepys begin in 1661 when he was not more than twenty-one or twenty-two. He was, says Dr. Johnson with characteristic disapproval and severity, " eager of the riotous and licentious pleasures which young men of high rank, who aspired to be thought wits, at that time imagined themselves entitled to indulge." Many of his pranks have been placed on record. They are neither very funny nor very edifying. On one occasion he and his brother Edward, with three friends, were committed to Newgate for killing an innocent man in a brawl, and should no doubt have been tried for murder, but as those contretemps could be arranged with very little difficulty the charge was modified to manslaughter.[1] On another occasion, the full details of which are not allowed to remain in the expurgated edition of Pepys, Lord Buckhurst, Sir Charles Sedley, and Sir Thomas Ogle got drunk at the Cock Tavern in Bow Street, where they went out on to a balcony, and Sedley took off all his clothes and harangued the crowd which collected below: the crowd, in indignation, drove them in with stones, and broke the windows of the house; for this offence all three gentlemen were indicted and Sedley was fined £500. On yet another occasion Buckhurst and Sedley spent the night in prison for brawling with the watch, and were delivered only on the King's intervention. On yet another, Pepys records that " the King was drunk at Saxam with Sedley and Buckhurst, the night that my Lord Arlington came thither, and would not give him audience, or could not." These and similar exploits recall the more celebrated escapade of Rochester as an astrologer, which at least had in it a humorous element entirely lacking in the mere rioting of drunken young men like Buckhurst and Sedley. It is not very surprising to learn that although he " inherited not only the paternal estate of the Sack-villes but likewise that of the Cranfields, Earls of Middlesex in right of his mother, yet at his decease his son, then only eighteen years of age, possessed so slender a fortune that his guardians when they sent him to travel on the Continent allowed him only eight

[1] The following account is abridged from the *Mercurius Publicus* of the day: "Charles Lord Buckhurst; Edward Sackville, his brother; Sir Henry Belasyse, eldest son of Lord Belasyse; John Belasyse, brother of Lord Faulconberg; and Thomas Wentworth, only son of Sir G Wentworth, whilst in pursuit of thieves near Waltham Cross, mortally wounded an innocent tanner named Hoppy, and . . . were soon after apprehended on charges of robbery and murder, but the Grand Jury found a bill for manslaughter only."

hundred pounds a year for his provision," nor that
" extenuated by pleasures and indulgences, he sank
into a premature old age." Before sinking into this old
age, however, he lived through the full enjoyment of a
splendid youth. It is difficult to imagine an era in
English history more favourable to a young man of
his type and fortune than the early years of Charles II,
when the King himself was the ringleader in the out-
burst of revolt against that iron-grey period of
Puritanism through which the country had just passed.
Dresses became extravagant, silver ornate, speech
licentious; the theatres, which had been closed for
over twenty years, reopened, the costumes and scenery
being now on an elaborate scale never contemplated
before; women—a daring innovation—appeared in
the women's rôles; the King and his brother patronised
the play-houses with all the young bloods of the court;
coaches clattered through the streets of London, yes,
even on a Sunday. There is, of course, another side
to the picture—the sullen disapproval of the serious-
minded, the squalor of a London shortly to be rotted
by plague and terribly purified by fire—but with this
side we have in the present connection no concern. We
are in the gay upper stratum of prosperity and fashion,
fortunate in the extraordinary vividness of our
visualisation; we know not only the principal charac-
ters, but also the crowd of " supers " pressing behind
them; we know their comings and goings, their
intrigues, their rivalries, their amusements, the names
of their mistresses. We are now at Whitehall, now at
Epsom, now at Tunbridge Wells, now at Richmond.
We are, indeed, very deeply in Pepys' debt.

In this world, therefore, so intimately familiar to
any reader of the great diarist, Lord Buckhurst moves

noisily with Rochester and Buckingham, Etherege and Sedley, " the first gentleman," says Horace Walpole, " of the voluptuous court of Charles II." We are told that he refused the King's offers of employment in order to enjoy his pleasures with the greater freedom, or, as he himself wrote with much frankness:

May knaves and fools grow rich and great,
  And the world think them wise,
While I lie dying at her feet
  And all the world despise.

Let conquering Kings new triumphs raise,
  And melt in court delights :
Her eyes can give much brighter days,
  Her arms much softer nights.

This did not prevent him from enrolling as a volunteer in the Dutch war of 1665, when he was present at a naval battle, and when the song which he was reported to have written on the eve of the engagement was brought to London and bandied from mouth to mouth about the town. Dr. Johnson shows himself sceptical as to this picturesque legend of the origin of the verses. " Seldom is any splendid story wholly true," he observes; and continues, " I have heard from the Earl of Orrery, that Lord Buckhurst had been a week employed upon it, and only re-touched, or finished it, on the memorable evening." However this may be, both song and story remain: I have told the story, and quote the song:

To all you ladies now at land
We men at sea indite ;
But first would have you understand
How hard it is to write :
The Muses now, and Neptune too,
We must implore to write to you,
  With a fa, la, la, la, la.

For though the Muses should prove kind
 And fill our empty brain,
Yet if rough Neptune rouse the wind
 To wave the azure main,
Our paper, pen and ink, and we,
Roll up and down our ships at sea,
  With a fa, la, la, la, la.

Then if we write not by each post,
 Think not we are unkind;
Nor yet conclude our ships are lost
 By Dutchman or the wind:
Our tears we'll send a speedier way,
The tide shall bring them twice a day,
  With a fa, la, la, la, la.

The King with wonder and surprise
 Will swear the seas grow bold,
Because the tides will higher rise
 Than e'er they did of old:
But let him know it is our tears
Bring floods of grief to Whitehall stairs,[1]
  With a fa, la, la, la, la.

Should foggy Opdam chance to know
 Our sad and dismal story,
The Dutch would scorn so weak a foe
 And quit their fort at Goree;
For what resistance can they find
From men who've left their hearts behind?—
  With a fa, la, la, la, la.

Let wind and weather do its worst,
 Be you to us but kind,
Let Dutchmen vapour, Spaniards curse,
 No sorrow we shall find:
'Tis then no matter how things go,
Or who's our friend, or who's our foe,
  With a fa, la, la, la, la.

[1] This refers to the frequent flooding of Whitehall Palace by an unusually high tide.

To pass our tedious hours away
  We throw a merry main,
Or else at serious ombre play ;
  But why should we in vain
Each other's ruin thus pursue ?
We were undone when we left you,
  With a fa, la, la, la, la.

But now our fears tempestuous grow
  And cast our hopes away ;
Whilst you, regardless of our woe,
  Sit careless at a play ;
Perhaps permit some happier man
To kiss your hand, or flirt your fan,
  With a fa, la, la, la, la.

When any mournful tune you hear
  That dies in every note
As if it sighed with each man's care
  For being so remote,
Think then how often love we've made
To you, when all those tunes were played,
  With a fa, la, la, la, la.

In justice you cannot refuse
  To think of our distress,
When we for hopes of honour lose
  Our certain happiness :
All those designs are but to prove
Ourselves more worthy of your love,
  With a fa, la, la, la, la.

And now we've told you all our loves,
  And likewise all our fears.
In hopes this declaration moves
  Some pity for our tears :
Let's hear of no inconstancy,
We have too much of that at sea—
  With a fa, la, la, la, la.

With this song—which is really very good of its kind, and, I think, deserves its fame—Pepys says that he " occasioned much mirth," although at the time of repeating it he was under the impression that it was written by three authors in collaboration. It seems to have achieved popularity, and was set to music, also a parody was written of it by Lord Halifax under the title " The New Court: Being an Excellent New Song to an old Tune of ' To all you Ladies now at hand ' by the Earl of Dorset," and of which the following is the opening verse:

> To all you Tories far from Court
> We Courtiers now in play
> Do write, to tell you how we sport
> And laugh the hours away.
> The King, the Turks, the Prince, and all
> Attend with us each Feast and Ball.
> With a fa, etc.

It is shortly after this battle that Nell Gwyn first appears in Lord Buckhurst's life. London's two theatres—the Duke's Theatre, near Lincoln's Inn Fields, and the King's Theatre, or, more familiarly, The Theatre, in Drury Lane—were then the great new resort and amusement, from the King and his brother in their boxes down to the rabble in the pit. Until the reign of Charles II the presence of the King in a common play-house was an unknown thing: such plays or masques as they had witnessed were always specially performed for them either in the halls or cock-pits of their palaces, but it now became the fashion for not only the King and the Duke of York, but also for the Queen to patronise the theatres. There were other innovations. The public was no longer satisfied with the makeshift scenery of pre-Commonwealth days, which had too often consisted of a placard hung upon a nail, " *A wood*," or " *A throne-room*," or whatever it might be. Nor were the dresses of the actors as careless as they had formerly been, but patrons of the stage would give their old clothes, which, if shabby, were no doubt still sufficiently magnificent to produce their effect at a distance. Even a step further in progress was the appearance of women on the stage, " foul and undecent women now, and never till now, permitted to appear and act," says Evelyn, full of indignation, " who, inflaming several young noblemen and gallants, became their misses and to some their wives, witness the Earl of Oxford, Sir R. Howard, Prince Rupert, the Earl of Dorset, and another greater person than any of them." A theatre of that day must have been a noisy, ruffling, ill-lighted place. The ceiling immediately above the pit was either open to the sky or else inadequately covered over, so that in the event of rain the whole of the pit was apt to surge into the dry parts of the theatre. The ladies in the audience, especially if the performance happened to be a comedy, sat for the most part in masks. The sallow face of the King, framed by the heavy curls, leered down over the edge of a box. In the body of the theatre lounged the bucks of the town, exchanging pleasantry and impudence with the orange-girls who were so indispensable a feature.

These orange-girls stood in the pit, crying " Oranges ! will you have any oranges ? " and were under the control of a superior known as Orange Moll, a famous figure of London theatre life. One may quote, to give some further idea of the relations between the young dandies and the orange-sellers, some of the stage directions in Shadwell's *True Widow*, in the fourth act, laid in the Playhouse, "Several young cox-combs fool with the orange-women," or "He sits down and lolls in the orange-wench's lap," or, "Raps people on the back and twirls their hats, and then looks demurely, as if he did not do it." Amongst these girls, at the beginning of her career, was Nell Gwyn, of whom Rochester wrote:

> . . . . *the basket her fair arm did suit,*
> *Laden with pippins and Hesperian fruit ;*
> *This first step raised, to the wondering pit she sold*
> *The lovely fruit smiling with streaks of gold,*

and who has come down to us as a figure full of dis-reputable charm, witty Nelly, pretty Nelly, Nelly whose foot was least of any woman's in England, Nelly who paid the debts of those whom she saw being haled off to prison, Nelly the pert, the apt, the kind-hearted, Nelly who " continued to hang on her clothes with her usual negligence when she was the King's mistress, but whatever she did became her." This merry creature said of herself that she was brought up in a brothel and served strong waters to gentlemen: it is probable that she was born in the Coal Yard at Drury Lane (now Goldsmith Street), and, wherever she may have been brought up, at a very early age she joined the orange-girls at the King's Theatre. In due time her looks and her wit attracted attention and she went on the stage. Pepys, who was evidently much taken with the " bold merry slut," leaves a particularly charming record of her one May day:

May 1st. To Westminster, in the way meeting many milkmaids with their garlands upon their pails, dancing with a fiddler before them ; and saw pretty Nelly standing at her lodgings door in Drury Lane in her smock sleeves and

THE SPANGLE ROOM

Derek Aa[...]

THE STONE COURT

bodice, looking upon one ; she seemed a mighty pretty creature.

This being in May (1657), when Nell was sixteen, and had already been acting for at least two years, in July of the same year the diarist was told, which troubled him, that " my Lord Buckhurst hath got Nell away from the King's House, and gives her £100 a year, so as she hath sent her parts to the house and will act no more."

> *None ever had so strange an art*
> *His passion to convey*
> *Into a listening virgin's heart*
> *And steal her soul away*

was sung of Buckhurst. He was then twenty-seven or so, Nell Gwyn sixteen, and together they kept " merry house " at Epsom. Pepys went down to Epsom one day and heard reports of their merriments: he pitied Nelly, exclaiming, " Poor girl !" and pitied still more her loss to the King's Theatre; but he does not expressly state whether he saw the pair or not. In any case, the housekeeping at Epsom did not continue for very long, for by August she was again acting in London, and Pepys had " a great deal of discourse with Orange Moll, who tells us that Nell is already left by my Lord Buckhurst, and that he makes sport of her, and swears she hath had all she could get of him." It would appear from this that Buckhurst, contrary to what has been said of him, did not sell Nell Gwyn to the King, for even Pepys, who would surely have been among the first and best informed, does not mention the King having " sent for Nelly " until January of the following year. I hope, therefore, that the charges of his having accepted bribes in exchange for Nelly may be exploded. A great many things were whispered

—that he had been promised the peerage of Middlesex, that he had been given a thousand pounds a year, that he had been sent on " a sleeveless errand " into France to leave the coast clear for the King, that he refused to give her up until he had been repaid for all the expenses she had entailed upon him. I do not think that such a Jewish spirit is at all in keeping with the rest of his character as we know it, with his generosity and general lavishness, nor does it seem probable that he would so have bargained with a king whose favour he was anxious to retain. By 1669 it is certain that Nell was definitely the King's mistress and all connection with Buckhurst over. But we find that years afterwards the house called Burford House, at Windsor, is granted by Charles II to Charles, Earl of Dorset and Middlesex, W. Chaffinch, Esq., and others, in trust for Ellen Gwyn for life, with remainder to the Earl of Burford, the King's natural son, in tail male; further, among the Knole papers is the original deed of 1683 appointing Lord Dorset her trustee and trustee to her son by Charles II; and, dated 1678, there is an allusion to her former lover in one of Nell's infrequent and ill-spelt letters: " My lord Dorseit apiers worze in thre months, for he drinks aile with Shadwell and Mr. Haris at the Duke's house all day long."

Nell Gwyn thus passed out of Lord Buckhurst's life, which she had so briefly entered, a well-assorted pair, I think, in every respect—he, idle, spoilt, heavy and magnificent; she, coarse, witty, feminine. There is a portrait of her at Knole, which I suppose was acquired by him, and I once happened to see a set of spoons in a loan exhibition which were catalogued as bearing the arms of Sackville with those of Nell Gwyn. The

Sackville shield was correct enough, but whether the other quarterings were the arms of Gwyn, or whether indeed the orange-girl was entitled to any heraldic device, I am, of course, unable to say.

§ iii

Pomp, wealth, and infirmities now began to take the place of brilliant youth and comparative irresponsibility. The frivolous Lord Buckhurst became Earl of Dorset and Middlesex, he succeeded to the estates of the Cranfields, he married, he was made Lord Chamberlain, he was given the Garter, and he had a fit of apoplexy in the King's bedroom. In order to recover his health he went abroad; his passport is at Knole, on yellow parchment, with the King's signature at the top:

Charles the *Second* by the Grace of God, etc., to all admirals, vice-admirals, captains of our ships at sea, governors, commanders, soldiers, mayors, sheriffs, justices of the peace, bailiffs, constables, customers, controllers, searchers, and all other our loving subjects whom it may concern, greeting :

Whereas our right trusty and right well-beloved cousin CHARLES Earl *of* Dorset *and* Middlesex hath desired our licence to go beyond the seas for recovery of his health, we are graciously pleased to condescend thereunto, and accordingly our will and pleasure is, and we do hereby require, that you permit and suffer the said Charles Earl of Dorset and Middlesex with six servants by name Richard Raphael, Robert Pennock, Thomas Bridges, — Solomon, John Carter, and Christopher Garner, also forty pounds in money, and all baggage, utensils, carriages, and necessaries to the said Earl belonging, freely to embark in any of our ports and from thence to pass beyond the seas without any let, hindrance, or molestation whatsoever. And you are likewise to permit the said Earl and his servants at their return back into this Kingdom to pass with like freedom, into the same, affording them [as there may be occasion] all requisite aid and furtherance as well going as returning. And for so doing this shall be your warrant.

Given at our court at Windsor, the 23rd day of *August* 1681, in the three and thirtieth year of our reign.

By his Ma^{ty's} Command,

L. JENKINS.

There is also a letter from one of the servants mentioned in the passport, saying that they had had a good passage to Dieppe, "except Mr. Raphael, who was kind to ye fishes."

There is another letter, from the Mr. Raphael in question, written home to Robert Pennock from Paris while on the same journey, saying that his Lordship wants the pond finished against the spring, orders the gardener to manure all the trees, and wishes Pennock to obtain a sure-footed nag, as his Lordship intends for the future only to make use of a saddle-horse between Copt Hall and London to prevent the pain of the gravel, of which infirmity his Lordship has lately been much troubled.

About this time he married. I have in my hands one of his love-letters, in faded ink; there is no date, no beginning, and no signature: it is superscribed "for the Countess of Falmouth," and enclosed is a lock of reddish-brown hair—most dead and poignant token— of surprising length when one considers the heavy wig which was to be worn over it.

I must beg leave that we may be a little earlier than ordinary at Hick's hall today, for tomorrow, i may be so miserable as not to see you ; besides i am in pain till i can clear some doubts that have kept me waking all night ; something i observed in your looks which shewed you had been displeased, at what i dare not ask ; but till i know i must suffer the torment of uncertain guessing; though i am pretty well assured i could not be concerned in it [more than in the trouble it gave you]; being so perfectly yours, that it will of necessity be counted your own fault if ever i offend you, since 'tis you alone have the government not only of all my actions but of my very thoughts, to confirm you in the belief of this truth i do from this moment give up to you all my pretences to freedom or any power over myself, and though you may justly think it below you to be owned the sovereign of so mean a dominion as my heart, i have yet confidence upon my knees to offer it you; since never any prince could boast of so clear a title, and so absolute power, as you shall ever possess in it.

We know a good deal about Lord Dorset's expenses and finances. We know that on the death of his mother he obtained an additional income of £1744 14s. 11d. a year from her estates. We know that thirty-four houses in the Strand were granted to him, and let as follows:

	£	s.	d.
23 houses at from £6 to £65 each	950	7	1
3 houses built by him and let at £90 each	270	0	0
Total	£1220	7	1

We know that twenty-four tenements east of Somerset House were granted to him for ninety-nine years at a yearly rent of £24 10s. 4d.—and that out of them he should have made £1768 a year, as witness the list I reproduce, taken from a manuscript at Knole, but either he or his bailiff must disgracefully have neglected his business, for on Lord Dorset's death many rents were found to be in arrear, one tenant's yearly rent of £30 having accumulated to the sum of £235 5s. 6d., or nearly eight years' owing, and another rent of £17 18s. 4d. had accumulated to arrears of £111

19*s*. 10½*d*. His servants' accounts, too, were in a state of confusion, and some of the wages unpaid up to three years.

Signs	Rent		
	£	s.	d.
The Rising Sun	64	0	0
7 Stars and King's Arms	60	0	0
	60	0	0
	110	0	0
Surgeon's Arms	60	0	0
The Golden Ball	60	0	0
„ „ Key	60	0	0
	60	0	0
Mitre	90	0	0
3 Golden [?]	90	0	0
Black Lion	90	0	0
Golden Fleece	40	0	0
	60	0	0
Golden [?]	48	0	0
Two Cats	60	0	0
	60	0	0
	70	0	0
Hen and Chicken	60	0	0
Spread Eagle, a Bath house	40	0	0
	13	0	0
3 Black Lions	60	0	0
The Angel	70	0	0
	55	0	0
The Dorset Arms Tavern	140	0	0
Swan	33	0	0
	55	0	0
Bull Head Tavern	24	0	0
The Dial	34	0	0
Ship and Bale	34	0	0
The Peacock	8	0	0
	1768	0	0

His total income for the year 1698–99 was £7650 4*s*. 3½*d*.—the curious accuracy of these sums does not seem to tally with the confusion to which I have referred—that is to say, about £40,000 of modern money. It may be interesting, while on this subject, to show some of the means common among the great nobles for filling their pockets. In 1697, for instance, we read that " My Lord Chamberlain Dorset has sold the keepership of Greenwich Park to the Earl of Romney " [James Vernon to Matthew Prior], and in the same year—this is when he was getting on in years and entirely withdrawing from politics—" Lord Dorset hath resigned his office of Lord Chamberlain to the Earl of Sunderland for the sum of ten thousand pounds," but where was this sum to come from ? not out of Lord Sunderland's pocket; no, but " *which his Majesty pays*." There was yet another method by which money might conveniently be raised : it is well illustrated by Dorset's petition regarding the dues on tobacco:

To the King's most Ex^t Ma^ty
The humble Petition of CHARLES Earl *of* Middlesex.
   Humbly Sheweth
   That by the act [for preventing planting of tobacco in England and for regulating the Plantation Trade] all ships that shall return from any of yr Maj^ties foreign plantations and not return to yr Maj^ties Kingdom of England, Dominion of Wales or Town of Berwick upon Tweed, and there pay the customs and duties . . . shall be confisable and their bonds forfeited. That the *Phenix* of London, Richard Pidgeon Commander and several other ships have . . . discharged merchandizes of the growth of yr Maj^ties Plantations, in yr Kingdom of Ireland, so that by law they are forfeited as by the said Act produceable may appear.
   May it therefore please yr Sacred Maj^ty to grant yr Petitioner all forfeitures as well past as to come on accompt of the said Act, with power to depute such

persons as he shall think fitting, to look upon and take care that no such abuses shall be in ye future.

[*Knole MSS.* 1671.]

To this petition I should like to add another, representing the other point of view, that of the unfortunate people who had the King's soldiers quartered upon them in intolerable numbers, and were, as it appears, not refunded for the expenses to which they had been put. I add this the more willingly, as Dorset was commonly reputed the friend of the poor, and it is said of him that " crowds of poor daily thronged his gates, expecting thence their bread. The lazy and the sick, as he accidentally saw them, were removed from the street to the physician, and not only cured but supplied with what might enable them to resume their former calling. The prisoner has often been released by my Lord's paying the debt, and the condemned been pardoned, through his intercession with the sovereign."

To the Right Honble CHARLES Earl *of* Dorset *and* Middlesex.

The humble petition of the Innholders and Alehouse Keepers in the parish of Sevenoaks in the county of Kent, Humbly Sheweth,

That your said petitioners have every year since ye coming of his present Majesty had either foot or horse quartered on them, even much beyond their neighbours . . . The said innkeepers are willing to serve their King and Country, but beyond their ability cannot, they therefore humbly pray that care may be taken for procuring their arrears due, or at least to prevent more soldiers coming on them, which they understand are, unless your Honour will stand in the gap . . .

[*Knole MSS.*]

Some of the foregoing papers, then, account for his income; we have also some notes as to his expenses.

To his servants he paid £8 to £10 a year for " ordinary men and maids." For beef he paid 2s. a stone; for mutton, 3d. a pound; pullets were 6d. each; a goose was 1s. 8d.; a pheasant, 1s.; a hare, 8d.; a tongue, 1s.; a partridge, 9d.; a pigeon, 3d.; a turkey, 2s. 6d.; a calf's head, 1s. 6d. A bushel of oysters cost him 4s. 6d.; a peck of damsons, 1s. Wheat cost him 7s. a bushel; salt, 5s. a bushel. For 130 walnuts he paid 1s. 6d., and for a dozen candles 5s. 6d.—a surprising price. We have also a detailed account of his cellar. For strong beer he paid 35s. a hogshead, and for small beer 10s. a hogshead. From July 1690 to November 1691 his total wine bill amounted to £598 19s. 4d., an alarming sum when we reflect that he was paying only 5s. 1d. for a gallon of red port, 6s. 8d. for a gallon of sherry, and 8s. for a gallon of canary. We are given the details entered in the cellar from August 1690 to January 1691; they are sufficiently formidable: 425 gallons of red port, 85 gallons of sherry, 72 gallons of canary, 63 gallons of white port, and a quart of hock. One wonders whether Lord Dorset was " laying down," or whether this quantity was adequate only to the six months shown on the account book.

Lord Dorset seems to have carried large sums of money about on his person, for the steward's account book at Knole shows a regular daily entry of 10s. for loose change to his Lordship, and when he was set upon by footpads near Tyburn they robbed him not only of his gold George, but also of forty or fifty pounds. This does not perhaps seem a very enormous sum for a wealthy man to carry, but it must always be remembered that in order to obtain the modern equivalent it is necessary to multiply by at least five.

Before leaving the Knole papers of this date—and there is much that I have regretfully discarded, many letters, for instance, regarding the election of Lord Buckhurst to the House of Commons, which throw interesting sidelights upon the methods of electioneering in the early days of Charles II—I should like to quote one letter of unknown authorship, relating to the Rye House Plot. The letter is addressed to Lord Dorset: it is unsigned and undated, but the date must be placed, by virtue of internal evidence, in July 1683, by reason of the reference to Captain Walcot who was tried on July 12th in connection with the plot.

The party that went for my Lord Essex found him in his garden gathering of nut-meg peaches, he was lodged in my Lord Feversham's lodgings, in Whitehall, and the next day, having not made use of the favour of pen and ink, so well as my Lord Howard hath, he was sent to the Tower.

My Lord Howard runs like a spout, fresh, and fresh he hath writ enough to hang himself, and 1 hundred more, and cried enough to drown himself, he hath cast his lodgings in Whitehall.

Sir John Burlace was brought before the Council yesterday, upon sending intelligence to my Lord Lovelace that there was a warrant against him. He stayed one night in the messenger's hands and was this morning bail for my Lord Lovelace, and both of them dismissed.

The enclosed is an account how far the Grand Jury hath proceeded, that little note hath the names of some of the Grand Jury.

None were tried this afternoon but Capt. Walcot who was cast by a most clear evidence being at several consults, the places all named, his raising of arms, his own letter to the King, and one of the consults was at the Vulture, Ludgate Hill, and Sheppard's House, he had very little to say for himself, but that the witnesses swore away his life to secure their own, he excepted against all Jury men that were of the lieutenancy and behaved himself with a great deal of decency and resolution. They had a declaration ready drawn by Goodenough so soon as ever the King was killed, and particular men appointed to murder the most considerable persons. Borne by name was to kill this Lord Keeper, and refused it because it looked like an unneighbourly thing, my Lord pulled off his hat and said Thank you, neighbour.

I find also, dated 1690, this curious vocabulary of thieves' slang scribbled on the back of some particulars relating to the appointment of a new incumbent for Sevenoaks. Unfortunately half the alphabet is missing:

Autem mort	a marryed woman
Abram	naked
abram-cour	a tatterdemalion
autem	a church
boughar	a cur
bouse	drink
bousing-ken	an ale-house
borde	a shilling
boung	a purse
bing	to goe
bing a wast	to goe away
bube	ye pox
buge	a dog
bleating-cheat	a sheep
billy-cheat	an apron
bite ye peter or Roger	steal ye portmantle
budge	one that steals cloaks
bulk and file	a pickpocket and his mate
cokir	a lyar
cuffin quire	a justice
crampings	bolts and shackles
chats	ye gallows
crackmans	hedges
calle ⎫ togeman ⎬ Joseph ⎭	a cloak
couch	to lye asleep

couch a hogshead	to goe to sleep
commission ⎱ mish ⎰	a shirt
cackling-cheat	a chicken
cassan	cheese
crash	to kill
crashing-cheat	teeth
cloy	to steal
cut	to speak
cut bien whydds	to speak well
cut quire whydds	to speak evill
confeck	counterfeit
cly ye jerk	to be whipt
dimber	pretty
damber	rascall
drawers	stockings
duds	goods
deusea vile	ye country
dommerer	a madman
darkmans	night or even
dup	to enter
tip me my earnest	give me my part
filch	a staffe
ferme	a hole
fambles	hands
fambles cheats	rings and gloves
fib	to beat
flag	a groat
fogus	tobacco
fencing cully	one that receives stolne goods
glimmer	fire
glaziers	eyes
granna	corne
gentry more	a gallant wench
gun	lip
gage	a pot or pipe
grunting-cheat	a sucking pig
giger	a dore
gybe	a passe
glasier	one that goes in at windows

gilt	a picklock
harmanbeck	a constable
heave a book	to rob a house
half berd	sixpence
heartsease	20 shillings
knapper of knappers	a sheep stealer
lightmans	morning or day
lib	to tumble
libben	an house
lage	water
libedge	a bed
lullabye-cheat	a child
lap	pottage
lucries	all manner of clothes
maunder	to beg
magery prater	an hen
muffling-cheat	a napkin
mumpers	gentile beggars [1]

§ iv

In 1685 Charles II died, and with him departed that devil-may-care existence into which Lord Dorset had fitted so readily and so well. He was no favourite with the new King; for one thing he had addressed verses in this vein to Lady Dorchester, mistress of James II:

> *Tell me, Dorinda, why so gay,*
> *   Why such embroidery, fringe, and lace ?*
> *Can any dresses find a way*
> *To stop th' approaches of decay,*
> *   And mend a ruined face ?*
>
> *Wilt thou still sparkle in the box,*
> *   Still ogle in the ring ?*
> *Canst thou forget thy age and pox ?*
> *Can all that shines on shells and rocks*
> *   Make thee a fine young thing ?*

[1] *See* Appendix.

He appears also at this time to have grown more serious in his outlook, for he disapproved of the new King so strongly as to have taken an active part in the accession of William III to the English throne. He was instrumental, indeed, in arranging the escape of Princess (afterwards Queen) Anne:

That evening [*says Macaulay*] Anne retired to her chamber as usual. At dead of night she rose, and, accompanied by her friend Sarah [Churchill] and two other female attendants, stole down the back stairs in a dressing-gown and slippers. The fugitives gained the open street unchallenged. A hackney coach was in waiting for them there. Two men guarded the humble vehicle. One of them was Compton, Bishop of London, the princess' old tutor ; the other was the magnificent and accomplished Dorset, whom the extremity of the public danger had roused from his luxurious repose. The coach drove instantly to Aldersgate Street . . . there the princess passed the night. On the following morning she set out for Epping Forest. In that wild tract [it is amusing to think of Epping as a wild tract]—in that wild tract Dorset possessed a venerable mansion [Copt Hall], the favourite resort, during many years, of wits and poets . . .

but Macaulay was evidently not in possession of, or else ignored (although it is difficult to believe that the incident would not have tempted his picturesque and vivid pen), the detail related by Dorset's grandson, Lord George Sackville, that

one of her Royal Highness' shoes sticking fast in the mud, the accident threatened to impede her escape ; but Lord Dorset, immediately drawing off his white glove, put it on the Princess' foot, and placed her safely in the carriage.

That Lord Dorset had no sympathy with popery is proved by this letter, which is among the Duke of Rutland's papers:

Lord Dorset last night [27th January 1688] while at supper at Lady Northampton's, received the following letter with cross on top :

+

'Twere pity that one of the best of men should be lost for the worst of causes. Do not sacrifice a life everybody values for a religion yourself despise. Make your peace with your lawful sovereign, or know that after this 27th of January you have not long to live. Take this warning from a friend before repentance is in vain ;

and it is apparent that he had not lost touch with his old friends of the Court of Charles II, for we find, in 1688, that he placed Knole at the disposal of the Queen Dowager (Catherine of Braganza),

without any consideration of rent, besides the sole use of his park, and if she makes any alterations to have timber out of his woods for that purpose. The Queen Dowager will consider the repairs of the Lord Dorset's house, which will amount to £20,000.

But whether she availed herself of the offer, for however short a period, I cannot say.

Lord Dorset was in favour with William III, and continued to hold his office of Lord Chamberlain until he resigned it in 1697. This was the date when he withdrew from all public life. His second wife had died six years before; Dorset himself was approaching sixty, and the excesses of his youth had long since begun to tell. The end of a life which opened with such gaiety and *éclat* offers a very sordid picture. From his portraits it is easy to see that he has grown heavy and apoplectic: his features are coarsened and swollen; his double chins hang in folds over his voluminous robes, his ruffles, and his ribbons. He could not hope to enjoy his life at both ends. Those

must have been good days when he got drunk with
Sedley, or kept house with Nelly at Epsom, or exchanged witticisms with the King in the passages at
Whitehall, or sat after supper round the dining-room
table at Knole with Dryden and Killigrew and
Rochester; but after running up the account the debt
had to be paid at last. It was all very well for Prior,
who owed him everything, to get gracefully out of a
difficulty by saying that he drivelled better sense than
most men could talk: the remainder of the account is
not pretty to contemplate. " A few years before he
died," is the story told by his grandson, Lord George
Sackville, " he married a woman named Roche of very
obscure connections, who held him in a sort of
captivity down at Bath, where he expired at about
sixty-nine." There is a contemporary letter, which
says, " My Lord Dorset owns his marriage with one
of his acquaintances, one of the Roches. Do you think
anyone will pity him ? " " She suffered few persons
to approach him during his last illness, or rather,
decay," Lord George's account continues, " and was
supposed to have converted his weakness of mind to
her own objects of personal acquisition. He was indeed
considered to be fallen into a state of such imbecility as
would render it necessary to appoint guardians, with a
view to prevent his injuring the family estate, but the
intention was nevertheless abandoned. You have no
doubt heard, and it is a fact, that with a view of ascer-
taining whether Lord Dorset continued to be of a sane
mind, Prior, whom he had patronised and always
regarded with predilection, was sent down to Bath by
the family. Having obtained access to the Earl, and
conversed with him, Prior made his report in these
words, " Lord Dorset is certainly greatly declined in

Derek Adkins

THE CARTOON GALLERY

KNOLE FROM THE AIR

his understanding, but he *drivels* so much better sense even now than any other man can *talk*, that you must not call me into court as a witness to prove him an idiot." Congreve, appropriating the gist of the remark, observed after visiting Dorset on his deathbed, " Faith, he slabbers more wit dying than other people do in their best health." Swift also, who was an intimate friend of Lady Betty Germaine and the Dorsets in the succeeding generation, remarks that Charles grew dull in his old age. Ann Roche, who guarded so jealously her ancient and mouldy bird of Paradise, managed to provide handsomely for herself under his will. He left her not only the house in Stable Yard, St. James, which was hers before her marriage, but also lands and messuages in Sussex, two beds with the furniture thereunto belonging in his house at Knole, the furniture of two rooms there, all the household linen there, and £500 to be increased to £20,000 if his son should die without issue. The marriage only lasted a short time, for in 1705 Lord Dorset died—old, enfeebled, and semi-imbecile.

It is not surprising to learn that he left a number of illegitimate children: we know of at least four for certain, and there was probably a fifth, a son, as it is difficult to account otherwise for the William Sackville who writes, signing a remarkably ungrammatical letter with a remarkably beautiful signature, to ask for money, as he has lately " gained the affection of a young lady," and this, he promises, will be " the last trouble that ever I shall give your Lordship; it would come very seasonable to my present circumstances who has been harassed and ruined by the fate of war this four years past and have done the government good service, and never rewarded as those that deserved it less has." The other four were daughters. There is a petition at Knole from one of them:

To the Right Hon. CHARLES Earl of Dorset and Middlesex, Lord Chamberlain of Their Majesties' Household, the humble petition of MARY SACKVILLE:

That it having pleased ye Almighty to lay his afflicting hand on your petitioner's husband and her two small children for a long time together, having nothing to live upon but his own hands' labour, which failing him during his sickness all his family have suffered thereby and been put to great straights and having received much of your Honour's charity, is now . . . [illegible] but hopes that your Lordship will consider it is the hand of accident that is hard upon her.

Your petitioner therefore humbly prays that your Honour will be pleased to bestow something on her this time that she may undergo her calamity with a little more cheerfulness and alacrity.

According to the will of this Mary Sackville, her circumstances must have improved, for she leaves £1000 " for the benefit of Katherine Sackville my sister or reputed sister who was born of the body of Mrs. Phillipa Waldgrave, deceased, my late mother or reputed mother." This will is dated 1684, so I should think the Katherine Sackville referred to is probably the " K. S." who was buried at Withyham, aged fourteen, in 1690—humble little initials among the Lady Annes and Lady Elizabeths who surround her. She had been provided for in Lord Dorset's will also:

To my natural daughter Katherine Sackville, alias Walgrave, £1000.

To my natural daughter Mary Sackville, alias Walgrave, £200, and £2000 before settled on her.

To my natural daughter An [sic] Lee, alias Sackville, the sum of £500.

It thus seems probable that these daughters were the children of two different mothers, Lee and Walgrave, Waldgrave, Waldegrave, as it was variously spelt. An agreement at Knole, dated 1674, provides for Phillipa Walgrave to receive interest on £1000 placed in Mr. Guy's hands by Lord Dorset, the interest on it to be paid to her yearly, and after her death to Mary Sackville until her marriage or until the age of 21, but if Mrs. Walgrave marries, the £1000 is to be paid to her. Another natural daughter, also named Mary, married Lord Orrery, but I do not know who was her mother.

§ v

He had been one of the most notorious libertines of the wild time which followed the Restoration. He had been the terror of the city watch, had passed many nights in the round house, and had at least once occupied a cell in Newgate. His passion for Nell Gwyn, who always called him her Charles the First, had given no small amusement and scandal to the town. Yet, in the midst of follies and vices, his courageous spirit, his fine understanding, and his natural goodness of heart, had been conspicuous. Men said that the excesses in which he indulged were common between him and the whole race of gay young Cavaliers, but that his sympathy with human suffering and the generosity with which he made reparation to those whom his freaks had injured were all his own. His associates were astonished by the distinction which the public made between him and them. " He may do what he chooses," said Wilmot, " he is never in the wrong." The judgment of the world became still more favourable to Dorset when he had been sobered by time and marriage. His graceful manners, his brilliant conversation, his soft heart, his open hand, were universally praised. No day passed, it was said, in which some distressed family had not reason to bless his name. And yet, with all his good nature, such was the keenness of his wit that scoffers whose sarcasm all the town feared stood in craven fear of the sarcasm of Dorset. All political parties esteemed and caressed him, but politics were not much to his taste. Had he been driven by necessity to exert himself, he would probably have risen to the highest posts in the state ; but he was born to rank so high and to wealth so ample that many of the motives which impel men to engage in public affairs were wanting to him. . . . Like many other men who, with great natural abilities, are constitutionally and habitually indolent, he became an intellectual voluptuary, and a master of all those pleasing branches of knowledge which can be acquired without severe application. He was allowed to be the best judge of painting, of sculpture, of architecture, of acting, that the court could show. On questions of polite learning his decisions were regarded at all the coffee houses as without appeal. More than one clever play which had failed on the first representation was supported by his single authority against the whole clamour of the pit and came forth successful at the second trial. . . .

Macaulay thus summarises his career and character, and I am led quite naturally to the consideration of one aspect of his life on which I have scarcely touched, and that is his connection with the men of letters of his day. The often-quoted saying, that Butler owed to him that the court tasted his *Hudibras*, Wycherley that the town liked his *Plain Dealer*, and that the Duke of Buckingham deferred the publication of his *Rehearsal* until he was sure that Lord Buckhurst would not rehearse it upon him again—this saying had much truth in it. It is better, I think, to quote the disinterested opinion of Macaulay rather than the panegyrics of Prior or Dryden, or any of the contemporary authors who stood too greatly in Dorset's debt for complete impartiality:

Such a patron of letters England had never seen [*says Macaulay*]. His bounty was bestowed with equal judgment and liberality, and was confined to no sect or faction. Men of genius, estranged from each other by literary jealousy or difference of political opinion, joined in acknowledging his impartial kindness. Dryden owned that he had been saved from ruin by Dorset's princely generosity. Yet Montague and Prior, who had keenly satirised Dryden, were introduced by Dorset into public life ; and the best comedy of Dryden's mortal enemy, Shadwell, was written at Dorset's country seat. The munificent earl might, if such had been his wish, have been the rival of those of whom he was content to be the benefactor. For the verses which he occasionally composed, unstudied as they are, exhibit the traces of a genius which, assiduously cultivated, would have produced something great. In the small volume of his works may be found songs which have the easy vigour of Suckling, and little satires which sparkle with wit as splendid as those of Butler.

One can, perhaps, scarcely agree with Macaulay in this estimate of Dorset's literary gifts. The songs he wrote are little more than easy specimens of conventional Restoration verse, and, for my part, I fail to find in them, with the exception of " To all you ladies now at land," any merit which was not shared by all the numerous song-writers of the day. It certainly cannot be claimed for him that he had any of the vigour, originality, or true poetic impulse of his great-great-grandfather, the old Lord Treasurer, and although it may be argued that the age of Elizabeth and the age of the Restoration differed totally in poetic conception and spontaneity I still do not admit that Dorset possessed those qualities which might have made up in one direction for those which were lacking in another. I have already quoted his sea-song, unquestionably the best thing he ever wrote, and, to give point to my argument, will quote two further songs, which may stand as typical examples, the first of his graceful but entirely artificial talent, the second of his satire which caused Rochester to say of him :

For pointed satire I would Buckhurst choose,
The best good man with the worst natured muse.

SONG

Phyllis, for shame, let us improve
A thousand different ways
Those few short moments snatched by love
From many tedious days.

If you want courage to despise
The censure of the grave,
Though Love's a tyrant in your eyes,
Your heart is but a slave.

My love is full of noble pride
Nor can it e'er submit
To let that fop, Discretion, ride
In triumph over it.

False friends I have, as well as you,
Who daily counsel me
Fame and ambition to pursue
And leave off loving thee.

But when the least regard I show
To fools who thus advise,
May I be dull enough to grow
Most miserably wise.

To CATHERINE SEDLEY [married Sir David Colyear]

Proud with the spoils of royal cully,
With false pretence to wit and parts,
She swaggers like a battered bully
To try the tempers of men's hearts.

Though she appear as glittering fine
As gems, and jets, and paints can make her,
She ne'er can win a breast like mine :
The Devil and Sir David take her.

The fugitive character of his own verses does not, however, in any way detract from his splendour as a patron. It is well known that Matthew Prior as a boy was found by him reading Horace in a tavern in West-minster, when, struck by his intelligence, Dorset sent the boy at his own expense to school until his election as King's Scholar. Prior in after years did not forget this kindness. His poems are dedicated to the son of his earliest patron, and there are, as students of Prior will remember, several amongst them especially written to members of Dorset's family, notably the " Lines to Lord Buckhurst [Dorset's son] when playing with a cat." The many letters from Prior to Lord Dorset, now in Lord Bath's possession, testify to the endurance of their friendship: one of these letters ends with a poem, which I quote, as I am under the impression that it is not included in any edition of Prior's works :

Spare Dorset's sacred life, discerning Fate,
And Death shall march through camps and courts in state,
Emptying his quiver on the vulgar great :
Round Dorset's board let Peace and Plenty dance,
Far off let Famine her sad reign advance,
And War walk deep in blood through conquered France.
Apollo thus began the mystic strain,
The Muses' sons all bowed and said Amen.

It is perhaps less commonly known that Dryden also owed, in another way, much to Dorset. The account is thus given by Macaulay:

Dorset became Lord Chamberlain, and employed his influence and patronage annexed to his functions, as he had long employed his private means, in encouraging genius and alleviating misfortune. One of the first acts which he was under the necessity of performing must have been painful to a man of so generous a nature, and of so keen a relish for whatever was excellent in arts and letters. Dryden could no longer remain Poet Laureate. The public would not have borne to see any papist among the servants of their Majesties; and Dryden was not only a papist, but an apostate. He had, moreover, aggravated the guilt of his apostacy by calumniating and ridiculing the Church which he had deserted. He had, it was facetiously said, treated her as the pagan persecutors of old treated her children. He had dressed her up in the skin of a wild beast, and then baited her for the public amusement. He was removed; but he received from the private bounty of the magnificent Chamberlain a pension equal to the salary which had been withdrawn.

Dryden, apparently, despite this generosity, continued to lament his ill-fortune, and his contemporary Blackmore, in a poem called *Prince Arthur*, satirises him in the character of *Laurus* for his assiduity at Dorset's doors—Dorset being the *Sakil* of the poem, Sackville in transparent disguise:

> *The poets' nation did obsequious wait*
> *For the kind dole divided at his gate.*
> *Laurus among the meagre crowd appeared,*
> *An old, revolted, unbelieving bard,*
> *Who thronged, and shoved, and pressed, and would be heard.*
>
> *Sakil's high roof, the Muses' palace, rung*
> *With endless cries, and endless songs he sung.*
> *To bless good Sakil Laurus would be first;*
> *But Sakil's prince and Sakil's God he cursed.*
> *Sakil without distinction threw his bread,*
> *Despised the flatterer, but the poet fed.*

It is true that in his *Essay on Satire*, which, like his *Essay on Dramatic Poetry*, is dedicated in terms of the most outrageous flattery to Dorset, Dryden makes full acknowledgement of the obligation:

I must ever acknowledge, to the honour of your Lordship and the eternal memory of your charity, that, since this revolution, wherein I have patiently suffered the ruin of my small fortune, and the loss of that poor subsistence which I had from two kings, whom I had served more faithfully than profitably to myself; then your Lordship was pleased, out of no other motive but your own nobleness, without any desert of mine, or the least solicitation from me, to make me a most bountiful present, which at that time, when I was most in want of it, came most seasonably and unexpectedly to my relief.

But I think there may be detected, even in this acknowledgment, the note of whining to which Macaulay, in the continuation of the passage I have quoted, draws attention. It is also related that Dryden, when dining with Dorset, found a hundred-pound note hidden under his plate. In a letter preserved at Knole, in Dryden's beautiful handwriting, he makes further acknowledgement, after proffering a petition on behalf of a friend who wished to obtain rooms in Somerset House:

. . . if I had confidence enough, my Lord, I would presume to mind you of a favour which your Lordship formerly gave me some hopes of from the Queen ; but if it be not proper or convenient for you to ask, I dare give your Lordship no further trouble in it, being on so many other accounts already your Lordship's most obliged obedient servant,

JOHN DRYDEN.

We know that Dryden was a constant visitor at Knole; we have even an anecdote of one of his visits. It is related that someone proposed that each member of the party should write an impromptu, and that Dryden, when the allotted time had expired, should judge between them. Silence ensued while each guest wrote busily, or laboriously, upon the sheet of paper provided: Dorset scribbled a couple of lines and threw it down on the table. At the end of the time the umpire rose, and said that after careful consideration he awarded the prize to their host; he would read out what his Lordship had written; it was: " I promise to pay Mr. John Dryden or order five hundred pounds on demand. DORSET."

It would be interesting to know who were the other members of the party; perhaps Tom Durfey, perhaps

Lady Dorset, who is described as " jeune, belle, riche, et sage," perhaps Rochester, whose portrait hangs in the Poets' Parlour—and I imagine the Poets' Parlour to have been the scene of this little incident, " a chamber of parts and players," says Horace Walpole, " which is proper enough in that house "—a portrait of a young man in a heavy wig, labelled " died repentant after a profligate life," as I, not understanding the long words, used to gabble off to strangers along with other piteous little shibboleths when showing the house. Certainly Shadwell was not there, for he and Dryden were at mortal enmity; Shadwell, his successor in the Laureate-ship, another friend and protégé of Dorset's, described by Dryden as being

> Round as a globe, and liquored every chink,
> Goodly and great, he sails behind his link.
> For all this bulk there's nothing lost in Og,
> For every inch that is not fool is rogue,

and who writes of Dorset that he was received by him as a member of his family, and furthermore, rather plaintively, in a letter at Knole, beseeching Lord Dorset's intervention, as " they have put Durfey's play before ours, and this day a play of Dryden's is read to them and that is to be acted before ours too."

Tom Durfey, whose portrait is upstairs in Lady Betty's room, painted in profile, with surely the most formidable of all hooked noses, was almost a pensioner at Knole, having his own rooms over the dairy, and is guilty of these execrable verses in praise of his second home:

THE GLORY OF KNOLE

> Knole most famous in Kent still appears,
> Where mansions surveyed for a thousand long years,
> In whose domes mighty monarchs might dwell,
> Where five hundred rooms are, as Boswell[1] can tell !

[1] The butler, not the biographer.

I do not think that Durfey can have been very greatly esteemed by his patron, nor yet on very intimate terms with him, but kept rather, contemptuously, as permanent rhymester to Dorset's little court, for another picture, small, obscure, but entertainingly intimate, shows him in humble company in the Steward's Room with Lowry, the Steward; George Allan, a clothier; Mother Moss, whoever she may have been; Maximilian Buck, the chaplain; and one Jack Randall. His name is certainly not one of the most illustrious among the many poets and writers represented on the walls of the Poets' Parlour—Edmund Waller, Matthew Prior, Thomas Flattman, John Dryden, William Congreve, William Wycherley, Thomas Otway, Thomas Hobbes, John Locke, Samuel Butler, Abraham Cowley, Nicholas Rowe, William Cartwright, Sir Kenelm Digby, Alexander Pope. And with this last name I come to the final tribute paid to the splendid Dorset —Pope's epitaph upon his monument in the Sackville chapel at Withyham:

> *Dorset, the grace of courts, the Muses' pride,*
> *Patron of arts, and judge of nature, died.*
> *The scourge of pride, though sanctified or great,*
> *Of fops in learning, and of knaves in state :*
> *Yet soft his nature, though severe his lay,*
> *His anger moral, and his wisdom gay.*
> *Blest satirist ! who touched the mean so true,*
> *As showed vice had his hate and pity too.*
> *Blest courtier ! who could King and country please,*
> *Yet sacred kept his friendships and his ease.*
> *Blest peer ! his great forefather's every grace*
> *Reflected and reflecting in his race,*
> *Where other Buckhursts, other Dorsets shine,*
> *And patriots still, or poets, deck the line.*

CHAPTER VII

Knole in the Early Eighteenth Century

LIONEL SACKVILLE
7th Earl *and* 1st
Duke *of* Dorset

§ i

THE first duke of Dorset remains to me, in spite of much reading, but an indistinct figure. I do not know whether the fault is mine or his. Perhaps he was a man of little personality; certainly he was lacking in the charm of his scapegrace father or of his frivolous great-nephew, the third duke. And yet he is a personage of some solidity: weighty, Georgian solidity. The epithets chosen by his contemporaries to describe him are all concordant enough, " a man of dignity, caution, and plausibility," " worthy, honest, good-natured," " he preserved to the last the good breeding, decency of manner, and dignity of exterior deportment of Queen Anne's time, never departing from his style of gravity and ceremony," " a large-grown, full person," and finally—the words come almost with the shock of being precisely what we were waiting for—" in spite of the greatest dignity in his appearance, he was in private the greatest lover of low humour and buffoonery." He was fitted, if I piece together rightly my scraps of evidence, to lead the life of a country gentleman, performing his duty towards his county, entertaining his friends, enjoying with them after dinner the low humour to which he inclined; rolling out his laughter in the Poets' Parlour, slapping his great thighs, and rejoining his wife afterwards in the spirit of affectionate domesticity which induced him to begin his letters to her " dear, dear, dear girl," or " my dear, dear Colly." He lived, says one account of him, after detailing his amiable qualities as a kind husband and father, " in great hospitality all his life, and he was so respected that when at Knole on Sundays the front of the house was so crowded with horsemen and carriages as to give it rather the appearance of a princely levee than the residence of a private nobleman." It was his misfortune that he was not allowed to remain leading this kind of life so much to his taste: " the poor Duke of Dorset," said Lord Shelburne, " was made by his son to commence politician at sixty." The local offices which he held were well suited to his disposition and abilities; the titles of *Custos Rotulorum, Lord Lieutenant of Kent, Constable of Dover Castle*, and *Lord Warden of the Cinque Ports* sit admirably upon his rather provincial dignity. He could discharge these offices while surrounding himself with friends, and keeping open house at Knole. He was surely happy at Knole, with the duchess and the duchess' friend Lady Betty Germaine installed in her two little rooms in a corner of the house, and the correspondence with Dean Swift, and the echoes of the Restoration reaching him in the shape of dedications from Prior and Pope, who had been his father's friends. He must have been happy superintending the building of the " ruins " in the park, in ordering the removal of the clock from the roof of the Great Hall to a safer place over Bourchier's oriel, in putting up the balustrade in the Stone Court, in adding to the picture-gallery his own full-length Kneller, painted in Garter robes—a dignified and ponderous addition—in continuing his father's kindly and contemptuous patronage of Durfey, in entertaining the Prince of Wales, in receiving the present of a pair of elk-antlers measuring 7 foot from tip to tip, in playing at cards with his wife and Lady Betty, in watching the bull-baiting in the park, in inspiring the following tribute on the occasion of his birthday:

> *Accept, with unambitious views,*
> *The tribute of a female muse ;*
> *Free from all flattery and art,*
> *She only boasts an honest heart ;*
> *An heart that truly feels your worth,*
> *And hails the day that gave you birth ;*
> *Of younger men let others boast,*
> *Since Dorset is my constant toast ;*
> *Nor need the gayer world be told*
> *That Dorset never can grow old ;*
>
> *And with unerring truth agree,*
> *There's none so young, so blithe as he,*
> *With sprightly wit his jokes abound,*
> *Well-bred, he deals good-humour round ;*
> *The maid forgets her fav'rite swain,*
> *When Dorset speaks, he fights in vain ;*
> *The lover too, do all he can,*
> *Strives, but in vain, to hate the man.*
> *With this kind wish I end my lays,*
> *Be ever young with length of days.*

or such appreciation of his Christmas hospitality as this:

> *Our liquor at all times to nature gives fire,*
> *Infuses new blood, and new thoughts can inspire.*
> *Your wife, she may scold, undaunted you'll sing,*
> *For he that is drunk is as great as a King.*
>
> *In the field, if all night you lie under a willow,*
> *The soft easy snow shall be your down pillow.*
> *There's nothing can hurt you without or within*
> *When you've beef in your belly and Punch in your skin*

It is true that certain discordant notes troubled from time to time this Georgian harmony. The house-steward killed the black page in the passage; and the duke's sons themselves were unsatisfactory; even the favourite son, Lord George, who was the apple of his father's eye, fell into disgrace and was court-martialled on a charge of disobedience and cowardice. " I always told you," said Lord John on hearing of this, " that George was no better than myself." This affair of the battle of Minden must have been a heavy blow to the duke, but although Lord George was not exonerated he retained all his father's doting affection. Still, the mud had been slung at him and not a little had stuck. The two other sons were a source of sorrow: Lord John, after devoting his youth to cricket, went off his head; and Lord Middlesex, the eldest of the three, was an altogether deplorable character, prompting these verses, based upon an old saying about the family:

> *Folly and sense in Dorset's race*
> *Alternately do run,*
> *As Carey one day told his Grace*
> *Praising his eldest son.*

> *But Carey must allow for once*
> *Exception to this rule,*
> *For Middlesex is but a dunce,*
> *Though Dorset be a fool.*

I quote the verses as they stand, though " dunce " seems scarcely the right description to apply to Lord Middlesex, that dissolute and extravagant man of fashion, who squandered large sums of money upon producing operas, that " proud, disgusted, melancholy, solitary man," whose conduct savoured so strongly of madness. Certain family characteristics appeared in him which had skipped his father, and his father and he, consequently and not unnaturally, were not on very good terms. The duke, indeed, did not know what to make of his eldest son and heir. " Upon my word, Mr. Cary," he said, when Mr. Cary asked him loudly at the play whether Lord Middlesex was to undertake the opera again next season, " I have not considered what answer to make to such a question." Both Lord Middlesex and Lord John being so unsatisfactory, Lord George was, and remained, his father's favourite. Lord George, in an even greater degree than his father, is an incongruity among the Sackvilles, a departure from type. In spite of all his mistakes, his misjudgments, and his misfortunes, he was a man of greater ability than most of them, of greater energy than the common run of his indolent and pleasure-loving race, of a further-reaching ambition. He did not begin life as the eldest son, coming in due course to be the head of the family, and languidly accepting the civil or diplomatic posts which were pressed upon him; such career as he had he made for himself. Unlike his predecessors or their descendants, he was neither an ambassador, a poet, nor a patron of art or letters—" I have not," he wrote, " genius sufficient for works of *mere imagination* "—but first a soldier and then a statesman, both disastrously. It is not my intention to go into the details of his public career; my ignorance is too great of the tangle of Georgian politics; nor am I qualified to discuss whether he did or did not disobey his orders at Minden, whether he was or was not largely responsible for the loss of America, whether he did or did not write the *Letters of Junius* ; such questions are treated in histories of the period. Nor can I deal with the enormous number of letters on political subjects written both by and to Lord George: I have looked into them more than once, and have come away merely bewildered by the cross-threads of home politics, by the names of remembered or forgotten statesmen, by the fall and reconstruction of Ministries, by the crises of Whigs and Tories. So I judge it best to leave Lord George alone, " hot, haughty, ambitious, and obstinate, a sort of melancholy in his look which runs through all the Sackville family," and to seek neither to blacken nor to whitewash his character. I scarcely regard him as one of the Sackvilles, perhaps because he broke away from the family traditions into unfamiliar paths, perhaps also because he earned his own peerage, inherited a large house of his own, and led an existence separate from Knole. Living at Knole among its portraits and its legends which grew into the very texture of one's life, it was, I suppose, inevitable that one should grow up with pre-conceived affections or indifferences, and for some reason Lord George never awakened my interest or my sense of relationship. He was a public character, not a relation.

§ ii

The early impressions of the first duke, who grew to be so pompous, stout, and good-natured, and whose three sons gave him in their several ways so much anxiety, are not unattractive. There is a picture of him as a little slim boy, with his sister and their pet fawn; and there is Lord George's own anecdote of his father's childhood:

My father, having lost his own mother, was brought up chiefly by the Dowager Countess of Northampton, his

M

grandmother. She being particularly acceptable to Queen Mary, that Princess commanded her always to bring her little grandson, Lord Buckhurst, to Kensington Palace, though at that time hardly four years of age, and he was allowed to amuse himself with a child's cart in the gallery. King William, like almost all Dutchmen, never failed to attend the tea-table every evening. It happened that her Majesty having one afternoon by his desire made tea, and waiting for the King's arrival, who was engaged on business in his cabinet at the other extremity of the gallery, the boy, hearing the Queen express her impatience at the delay, ran away to the closet, dragging after him the cart. When he arrived at the door, he knocked, and the King asking " Who is there ? " " Lord Buck," answered he. " And what does Lord Buck want with me ? " replied his Majesty. " You must come to tea directly," said he, " the Queen is waiting for you." King William immediately laid down his pen and opened the door. Then taking the child in his arms, he placed Lord Buckhurst in the cart, and seizing the pole drew them both along the gallery to the room in which were seated the Queen, Lady Northampton, and the company. But no sooner had he entered the apartment, than, exhausted with the effort, which had forced the blood upon his lungs, and being constitutionally asthmatic, he threw himself into a chair, and for some minutes was incapable of uttering a word, breathing with the utmost difficulty. The Countess of Northampton, shocked at the consequences of her grandson's indiscretion, would have punished him, but the King intervened on his behalf.

When a young man he went on the inevitable Grand Tour. This journey, it is fair to assume, which was taken at the instigation of his mother's relations, was designed to keep him away from the influence of his enfeebled father and of his step-mother, Ann Roche, quite as much as for the benefit of his education. His father was very angry at this withdrawal of his son from his authority, and wrote to him:

i hear my Lady Northampton has ordered you not to obey me ; if you take any notice of what she says i have enough in my power to make you suffer for it beyond what she will make you amends for. But i cannot imagine you to be such a fool as to be governed by the passion and folly of anybody.

Your affectionate father,

DORSET.

i expect you will come away by the next yocht.

The next yacht, however, came away without Lord Buckhurst, and the young man did not return to England until after his father's death. Shortly after his succession and return he married Elizabeth Colyear, his " dear, dear Colly," and was appointed Lord Warden of the Cinque Ports at a salary of £160 a year, and Lieutenant of Dover Castle at £50. This is the menu and cost of the dinner given by the youthful Lord Warden at Dover Castle on the 16th August 1709 on his being appointed by Queen Anne:

	£	s.	d.
5 Soups	3	0	0
12 dishes of fish	10	16	0
1 Westphalia Ham and five fowls	1	6	0
8 dishes of pullets and oysters, with bacon	4	16	0
10 Almond Puddings	3	0	0
12 haunches of venison, roast	1	16	0
6 dishes of roast pigs	2	2	0
3 dishes of roast geese	1	4	0
12 Venison pasties	6	0	0
12 white Fragacies with Peetets	7	4	0
8 dishes of " ragged " veal	4	16	0

Second Course

	£	s.	d.
14 dishes of ducks, turkeys, and pigeons	8	0	0
15 codlin tarts, creamed	4	10	0
12 dishes of roast lobster	4	16	0
12 dishes of umble pies	4	4	0
10 dishes of fried fish	5	0	0
8 dishes of Chickens and rabbits	4	0	0

Ryders	£	s.	d.
5 dishes of dried sweetmeats	17	10	0
12 dishes of jelly	4	16	0
6 dishes of Selebub cream	2	8	0
13 dishes of fruit	10	0	0
8 dishes of Almond Pies gilt	4	16	0
12 dishes of Custard Florentines	3	12	0
8 dishes of lobster	3	4	0
120 Intermediate plates of sorts	9	0	0

Side-Table

	£	s.	d.
A large chine of beef stuck with flags and banners	5	10	0
1 loaf of double refined sugar	0	4	6
Oil and vinegar	0	3	0
Outcharges and expenses of pewter, carriage, bread, wharfage, turnspits, glasses, mugs, for ten men, horses, use of bakehouse, cooks, coach hire	76	16	9

This was an office he held intermittently for many years, and on one occasion, England being then at war with Spain, two hundred and fifty butts, eight hogsheads, and fifty quarter casks of Spanish mountain wine, and one hundred jars of Raisins of the Sun, being washed up at Deal and Sandwich, they were adjudged to him as the Lord Warden's perquisite of flotsam and jetsam.

In 1714 died Queen Anne, and Lord Dorset, with others, was sent to Hanover to announce to George his accession to the English throne. He returned from Hanover with the new King, and drove with him in his coach from Greenwich to London. On the way George related that thirty-three years earlier he had travelled to England as a suitor for the hand of Queen Anne: returning to Gravesend after the failure of his mission, he rode a common post-horse, which gave him a fall, so that he arrived at Gravesend covered with mud. The King amused himself in the coach with looking out for the place where this misfortune had come upon him, and pointed it out to Lord Dorset, who no doubt joined politely in the laughter.

Thus began that curious reign of a King who did not know the language of his adopted country, who spent as much time in his Hanoverian as in his English estates, and infinitely preferred them, who surrounded himself with German courtiers and mistresses, and who locked up his wife for two-and-thirty years as a punishment for her infidelity. The solemnity of Lord Dorset cannot have been out of place in such a court. Honours now crowded rapidly upon him, although at one moment he was temporarily deprived of all his offices for taking part in political intrigues. He was made a Knight of the Garter, six years later he was made a duke, he was given the office of Lord Steward, and finally he entered upon the first lap of his unfortunate career as Lord Lieutenant of Ireland. Before this, however, he was for the second time called upon to be the bearer of news of accession to a King of England. I give the account in Lord George's words:

When the intelligence of his [George I's] decease, which took place near Osnabrugh, in the end of July 1727, arrived in London, the Cabinet having immediately met, thought proper to dispatch the Duke of Dorset with the news to the Prince of Wales. He then resided at Kew, in a state of great alienation from the King, the two Courts maintaining no communication. Some little time being indispensable to enable my father to appear in a suitable manner before the new monarch, he sent forward the Duchess his wife, in order to announce the event. She arrived at Kew just as the Prince, according to his invariable custom, having undressed himself after dinner, had laid down in bed. The Duchess demanding permission to see him immediately, on business of the greatest importance, the servants acquainted the Princess of Wales with her arrival; and the Duchess, without a moment's hesitation, informed her Royal Highness, that George the First lay dead at Osnabrugh, that the Cabinet had ordered her husband to be the bearer of the intelligence to his successor, and that the Duke would follow her in a short time. She added that not a moment should be lost in communicating so great an event to the Prince, as the Ministers wished him to come up to London that same evening, in order to summon a Privy Council, to issue a proclamation, and take other requisite measures, at the commencement of a new reign.

To the propriety of all these steps the Princess assented; but at the same time informed the Duchess, that she could not venture to enter her husband's room, as he had only just taken off his clothes and composed himself to sleep. "Besides," added she, "the Prince will not give credit to the intelligence, but will exclaim that it is a fabrication, designed for the purpose of exposing him." The Duchess continued nevertheless to remonstrate with her Royal Highness, on the injurious consequences of losing time, and adding that the Duke of Dorset would expect to find the Prince not only apprised of it, but ready to accompany him to London. The Princess of Wales took off her shoes, opened the chamber door softly, and advanced up to the bedside, while my mother remained at the threshold, till she should be allowed to enter the apartment. As soon as the Princess came near the bed, a voice from under the clothes cried out in German, *Was ist das?* "I am come, sir," answered she, "to announce to you the death of the King, which has taken place in Germany." "That is one damned trick," returned the Prince, "I do not believe one word of it." "Sir," said the Princess, "it is most certain. The Duchess of Dorset has just brought the intelligence, and the Duke will be here immediately. The Ministers hope that you will repair to town this very evening, as your presence there is indispensable." Her Royal Highness then threw herself on her knees, to kiss the new King's hand; and beckoning to the Duchess of Dorset to advance, she came in likewise, knelt down, and assured him of the indisputable truth of his father's decease.

Convinced at length of the fact, he consented to get up and dress himself. The Duke of Dorset arriving in his coach and six, almost immediately afterwards, George the Second quitted Kew the same evening for London.

George the Second, as Prince of Wales, had been on terms of personal friendship with the duke. He had stayed at Knole, when half an ox, four sheep, and a calf were provided, besides the following items for his visit:

	£	s.	d.
Butcher	17	0	0
Bread and flour	4	0	0
Fowls, butter and eggs	14	15	0
Poulterer	11	14	0
Fishmonger	9	4	0
Confectioner	25	10	0
Wine	66	0	0
Beer	35	0	0
Master-cook's bill	20	9	0
To the cooks	37	12	6
The pewterer	3	12	4
The carrier	9	0	0
Lord Lumley's Grenadiers	3	4	6
	£257	1	4

The duke's first essay in Ireland was not unsuccessful : he left affairs alone as far as he possibly could and was tolerably popular. It was only the second time, twenty years later, that he and Lord George incurred so much dislike. Into the political reasons for this I have already said that I will not, because I cannot, enter ; I will only quote from a curious lampoon, preserved in the British Museum, which was written to celebrate the duke's departure in 1754:

𝕽𝖎𝖓𝖌𝖎𝖓𝖌 𝖔𝖋 𝖙𝖍𝖊 𝕭𝖊𝖑𝖑
or
A *Hue* & *Cry* after *Raymond* the *Fox*

By ROGER SPY, Esq.

The bells are ringing, Hark! how they merrily toll. What is the cause of their joy? Or why this cheerful tintinnation? They seem animated, and their rejoicing seems sensible, so expressive of triumph and hilarity are their peals, treble, bass and tenor make excellent harmony, and strike the very heart; the ringers themselves pull with pleasure—what is it they toll forth, or what may the bells be supposed to say?

Interpreter

I'll tell you what they say . . .

St. Patrick's

He was full of Pa-pa tricks,
Says the bell of St. Patrick's.

St. Mary

I wonder how dare he,
Says the bell of St. Mary.

St. Bride

Our acts he belied,
Says the bell of St. Bride.

St. Ann

He played Cat-in-Pan,
Says the bell of St. Ann.

St. Andrew

Bad swash as e'er man drew,
Says the bell of St. Andrew.

St. Peter

No vinegar sweeter,
Says the bell of St. Peter.

St. Owen
In mischief full knowing,
Says the bell of St. Owen.

St. Thomas
The Lord keep him from us,
Says the bell of St. Thomas.

St. Nicholas Without
He put good men out,
Says St. Nicholas Without.

St. Nicholas Within
He put bad men in,
Says St. Nicholas Within.

Castle Bell
You're a very bad parcel,
Says the bell of the Castle,

and so on, in the same vein.

His patronage of the actress Peg Woffington sets him in a more personal and amiable light. I have no evidence to prove whether he was following in the steps of his father; I only know that Peg Woffington's portrait, like that of Nell Gwyn and of the Baccelli, is at Knole; that an old play-bill of hers was found behind the panelling in the Great Hall; that the duke gave her a command performance at Dublin; and, finally, that the following facetious petition—was it written by one of the duke's disrespectful sons?—is among the Knole papers:

To his Grace L I O N E L Duke *of* DORSET, Lord Lieu^t *of* Ireland

The humble Memorial of MARGARET WOFFINGTON, *Spinster.* Most humbly sheweth

That your Memorialist is a woman of great merit and

165

small fortune, and would be proud of an opportunity of shewing her zeal for his Majesty's service by her ready acceptance and faithful discharge of any employment he shall graciously please to bestow upon her.

That her friends have been at great expense and trouble in procuring and perusing the list of the several places on this establishment, and find her extremely well qualified to discharge the Office of Housekeeper to his Majesty's Castle as it doth not require much greater ability than the Rolls or the Chancellorship of the Exchequer.

That your Memorialist is a true friend to the present Constitution in opposition to all Mock Patriots and drinks the Brownlow Majority and the Minority for the Money-bill every day devoutly.

That she has already by the assistance of whisky made two considerable Proselytes Patrick O'Donoghoe and Thady Foley her Chairman tho' one of them had been closeted by Col. Dilkes and the other taken by the hand by Sir Richd Cox, and verily believes if the same means were employed, the Opposition would soon lose its principal supporters.

That your Memorialist can produce two of the greatest Polemical Writers of the present Age in support of her character. 1st. Peter Willson who has abused her more than once in his *Universal Advertiser*—an honour which he is never known to confer on any but persons of the first ranks and character. 2dly Geo. Faulkner, in whose impartial Journal are contained a Score of Poems, One Dozen of Sonnets, Six letters from some of the best Critics, if you will take their own words for it, four Epigrams, besides occasional paragraphs, all composed in her praise, and which are at least as well written as they are printed.

That your Memorialist is little versed in the House-keeper's Arithmetic, having never been instructed in the doctrine of Items, Dittos, Sums Total and Balances, which circumstance, it is conceived, will turn out greatly to the advantage of the Government.

That her personal attachment to your Grace is so well known, that odd reports have been raised in relation to some intimacies that have past between two persons that shall be nameless, and which she defies her adversaries to prove.

Wherefore she humbly hopes that Your Grace will take the premises into your serious consideration, and oblige the present Incumbent to resign the said office, your Memorialist paying her the full value thereof, or if she continues obstinate as old women are apt to do, and refuses to sell, that the reversion may be granted to your Petitioner, and the rather as she conceives, if it be not done under your Grace's administration, there may be some reason to fear it will never be done at all.   MARGARET WOFFINGTON.

Mem : She is ready and willing to act as first Chambermaid to your Grace, to warm your bed and tuck you in, which, as she is advised and verily believes, the present Housekeeper is in no manner qualified to do.

§ iii

I have already mentioned Lady Betty Germaine, who, during the lifetime of the first duke and duchess, lived almost entirely at Knole and had three rooms—her bedroom, her sitting-room, and her china closet—set aside for her exclusive use. This little prim lady, to whom the three little rooms must have provided so apposite a frame, occupied her time in writing letters, in stitching at crewel work with brightly-coloured wools, in making pot-pourri to fill the bowls on the window ledges, and in telling anecdotes of Queen Anne, whose lady-in-waiting she had once been, since to her, no doubt, in common with all human nature, the days which were the past were preferable to the days which were the present. She was, primarily, the friend of the Duchess of Dorset, and for once a woman was installed in the house whose coiffure and petticoats the wind of scandal was unable to ruffle. They composed she, the duchess, the duke, and Lord George, a harmonious quartette, whose correspondence survives, voluminous and intimate, pricked into sharper highlights here and there by the pen of Swift. " As to my duchess," writes Lady Betty, " she is so reserved that perhaps she may not be at first so much admired." The duke she thought " great-souled," and it must have been an occasion of great distress to her that her friend Swift should not always share her views:

Madam [*he writes to her after failing to obtain some favour from Dorset*], I owe your Ladyship the acknowledgement of a letter I have long received, relating to a request I made to my Lord Duke. I now dismiss you, Madam, from your office of being a go-between upon any affair I might have with his Grace. I will never more trouble him, either with my visits or application. His business in this kingdom is to make himself easy ; his lessons are all prescribed for him from Court ; and he is sure, at a very cheap rate, to have a majority of most corrupt slaves and idiots at his devotion. The happiness of this Kingdom is of no more consequence to him than it would be to the Great Mogul . . .

One wonders whether such suggestions troubled Lady Betty. Was it possible that her great-souled friend would not be Lord Steward and Lord Lieutenant of Ireland and Lord Warden and Lord Lieutenant of Kent, did he not also happen to be Duke of Dorset ? Was it possible that people such as the Sackvilles occasionally occupied positions due to their birth rather than to their intellect ? Was it true that he, and particularly Lord George, cared for their own advancement rather than for the credit of England ? —they who *were* England, who shared the blood of the Tudors and the Howards and the Spencers and the Cliffords ? whose house was quarried from Kentish rock ? whose oaks and beeches were rooted so deep into the soil of England ? Lady Betty herself, who as Lady Betty Berkeley had come from that most ancient castle—that rose-and-grey castle, the colour of her own dried rose-leaves, the castle that, squat, romantic, and uncouth, brooded over the Severn across the meadows of Gloucestershire—Lady Betty herself was of all people least qualified or likely to criticize. The household at Knole was ordered on a magnificent scale, with the duke and duchess and their guest at the apex of the pyramid which reposed on the base of five servants at £20 each, two at £15, two at £10 10s., seven at £10, two at £8, thirteen at £6, eight at £5, two at £5, one at £2, besides the chaplain who was unsalaried, the senior officers, the Steward, the Comptroller, and the Master of the Horse at £60, £30, and £25 respectively, Tom Durfey living over the dairy, and the rabble of labourers, gardeners, and what-not, of whom nobody took any notice. This was life as Lady Betty was accustomed to find it ordered. If ever she paused to question its system, no trace of her wondering appears in her letters.

She had a house of her own, Drayton, in Northamptonshire, considered by Horace Walpole a " venerable heap of ugliness, with many curious bits," which she had inherited from her late husband, who in his turn had inherited it from a first wife. This husband of Lady Betty's is a peculiar figure; so peculiar, indeed, so ambiguous, and so equivocal, that one wonders at his alliance with the orderly Lady Betty Berkeley, unless this may be explained by the fact that he " possessed a very handsome person, and was always a distinguished favourite of the other Sex." He was, I gather, a soldier of fortune, of uncertain parentage, or, as Lord George Sackville delicately puts it, " believed to stand in a very close degree of consanguinity to King William the Third." William, at any rate, brought him over to England from Holland in 1688, knighted him, saw to it that he became a member of the House of Commons, and assisted him with grants of money; and Germaine, who inherited from his father no armorial bearings, was accustomed to use a red cross, which might be taken to mean that his actual was higher than his ostensible birth. This gentleman combined with the instincts of a collector a profound ignorance of artistic matters. His principal pride was his collection of " Rarities," in which he would exhibit the dagger of Henry VIII; he believed a certain Sir Matthew Germaine to be the author of St. Matthew's Gospel; and at Drayton, where he was building a colonnade, he caused the columns to be placed upside down, as he had mistaken the capitals for the pedestals.

This was the man who married Lady Betty Berkeley when she was thirty years younger than himself. He had previously been married to the Duchess of Norfolk, whose husband divorced her on Sir John Germaine's account. After her death, by which he inherited Drayton, he attached himself to the Duke and Duchess of Dorset, who received him with their wonted hospitality; but this was not enough : he wanted a brilliant alliance, he wanted an heir to Drayton. While at Bristol he " cast his eyes upon Lady Betty, whose birth, character, and accomplishments rendered her every way worthy of his choice." They married; and the friendship with the Dorsets, to whom Lady Betty was already devoted, was strengthened by the new bond. Although the difference in age was so considerable, Lady Betty, through her " superior understanding, added to the most correct deportment, acquired great influence over him," and when after twelve years of marriage Sir John died, " a martyr to the gout as well as to other diseases," he called his wife to his bedside and spoke to her in these terms:

Lady Betty [*said he*], I have made you a very indifferent husband, and particularly of late years, when infirmities have rendered me a burden to myself, but I shall not be much longer troublesome to you. I advise you never again to marry an old man, but I strenuously exhort you to marry when I am gone, and I will endeavour to put it in your power. You have fulfilled every obligation towards me in an exemplary manner, and I wish to demonstrate my sense of your merits. I have, therefore, by my will, bequeathed you this estate, which I received from my first wife ; and which, as she gave to me, so I leave to you. I hope you will marry and have children to inherit it. But, if events should determine otherwise, it would give me pleasure to think that Drayton descended after your decease to a younger son of my friend the Duchess of Dorset.

He then passed away, but in one particular Lady Betty did not take his advice: she never married again, although she survived him by fifty years, and thus it is perhaps that I regard her, with her crewel work, her china closet, and her pot-pourri, rather as a spinster than as a widow. There is no trace at all at Knole of Sir John Germaine, that royal bastard, that handsome and enterprising child of fortune, thanks to whom Drayton came into the possession of Lord George and continues to this day in the hands of his descendants. Of Lady Betty, on the other hand, there are copious traces. There are her rooms, which I have already described in the first chapter, her small square four-poster, her ring-box, and the painted wooden figure of a lady with the *fontange* of Queen Anne's day on her head. There is Lady Betty's own portrait, a miniature full-length, in blue brocade. There is yard upon yard of her industrious embroidery. There is the pot-pourri which is made every summer from her receipt (1750):

Gather dry, Double Violets, Rose Leaves, Lavender, Myrtle flowers, Verbena, Bay leaves, Rosemary, Balm, Musk, Geranium. Pick these from the stalks and dry on paper in the sun for a day or two before putting them in a jar. This should be a large white one, well glazed, with a close fitting cover, also a piece of card the exact size of the jar, which you must keep pressed down on the flowers. Keep a new wooden spoon to stir the salt and flowers from the bottom, before you put in a fresh layer of bay salt above and below every layer of flowers. Have ready of spices, plenty of Cinnamon, Mace, Nutmeg, and Pepper and Lemon-peel pounded. For a large jar ½ lb. Orris root, 1 oz. Storax, 1 oz. Gum Benjamin, 2 ozs. Calamino Aromatico,[1] 2 grs. Musk, and a small quantity of oil of Rhodium. The spice and gums to be added when you have collected all the flowers you intend to put in. Mix all well together, press it down well, and spread bay salt on the top to exclude the air until the January or February following. Keep the jar in a cool, dry place.

In the second respect Lady Betty carried out her husband's wishes, for when she died herself at the age of nearly ninety she bequeathed the " venerable heap of ugliness " to Lord George, with £20,000 and half the residue of her estate.

§ iv

CHARLES SACKVILLE
2nd
Duke *of* Dorset

Since I have avoided all political details, which would have led anyone more conversant than myself with the background to the facts into pages of dis-

[1] The powdered dried root of Sweet Sedge (*Acorus Calamus*).

Geo. P. King

JOHN FREDERICK SACKVILLE, 3rd Duke of Dorset, 1745–1799
From the portrait at Knole by Thomas Gainsborough

LADY BETTY GERMAIN, 1680–1769
From the portrait at Knole by C. Philips

sertation, there remains very little to say of the first Duke of Dorset. He died a few years before his dear, dear Colly, and was succeeded by his son, that Lord Middlesex to whom I have alluded as being so unsatisfactory. There is not much record of this good-for-nothing duke, who enjoyed his dukedom only four years, and who was married to a " very short, very plain, very yellow, and vain girl, full of Greek and Latin." Apparently he married her no earlier than he need, for Horace Walpole writes of " Lord Middlesex's wedding, which was over a week before it was known. I believe the bride told it then, for he and all his family are so silent that they would never have mentioned it; she might have popped out a child, before a single Sackville would have been at the expense of a syllable to justify her." I have already quoted the few epithets I have found relating to this duke, the "proud, disgusted, melancholy, solitary man . . ." who produced operas and spent enormous sums on defending singers in legal actions. He was reputed mad, "a disorder which there was too much reason to suppose, ran in the blood "; he was certainly eccentric; and there is a large picture of him in the ball-room at Knole dressed as a Roman emperor, with bare knees, a plumed helmet on his head, and various pieces of armour. Besides these scanty documents, there are some verses which scarcely entitle him to be called a poet: *Arno's Vale*, which I have never read, and which is addressed to a certain Madame Muscovita, whose portrait is at Knole; and others which are at Knole, for instance:

DUCK HUNTING

Hard by where Knole's exalted towers rise
Upon a green smooth plain a pond there lies,

With verdant grass encircled round, a place
Seated commodiously the duck to chase.
Here in the heat of day the youths for sport
With well-taught spaniels to the pond resort.
The youths on ev'ry side the pond surround,
With fav'ring cries the hollow woods resound.
The eager dogs with barking rend the skies
Until encouraged by their masters' cries
They plunge into the stream : the stream before 'em flies.
Rover, the first that plung'd, the first in fame
And one from Charles's noble breed that came.
The next came Trip, tho' of a bastard race,
And smaller size, he swam the next in place.
The last came Ranger, with his spotted back,
That swam but slow : the gravest of the pack.
His deep rough voice was of a hoarser sound
With long red ears that swept along the ground. . . .
And thus the sport goes on, till weary grown,
And ev'ryone is willing to go home.
The weary duck at last swims close to land ;
They take her up with a kind, pitying hand.
Of every spannel they extoll the praise
And all their virtues to the skies they raise.
And then they, weary, homewards take their way,
And drown in sprightly bowls the labours of the day.

The duke's poems are worthless, of course, but
among the Knole papers of this date is one which I
cannot forbear from reproducing :

AN EPISTLE *from* DAME I . . . L . . . . *to the*
REVD. MR. B . . .

Sweet youth, 'tis hard thy innocence should be
A source of scandal and reproach to me.
Nay, blush not—with reluctance I prevail
O'er innate modesty to own the tale.

That fatal day when first I saw thy face
And marked each angel-look and smiling grace,
Thy fair idea struck my tender heart,
And, oh! remained, though thou didst soon depart;
Maternal love, methought, thou didst inspire,
Around my heart still played the lambent fire.
Thoughtless of harm, why should I aught conceal?
A friend I meet, and thus the truth reveal:

" Say, didst thou mark that dove-like form to-day,
Those eyes that languished with so mild a ray?
Can fleecy lambs such innocence disclose,
E'er glowed such blushes on the opening rose?
Safe could I take the youngster to my bed
And on my bosom fondly rest his head,
Harmless the tedious night were so beguiled;
So watch fond mothers o'er the sucking child."

That seeming friend betrayed me, and began
To whisper through the house, " I loved the man."
Then memory spread and worse suspicions rose,
And searching spies broke in on my repose;
Nor chamber, closet, bed, were sacred then:
They sought to find thee, ah! they sought in vain!
Thou wrapped in innocence might sleeping be,
Unconscious of the woes I bore for thee.

The uproar now withdrawn, I strive to rest,
And throw my arms across my pensive breast.
Soon as my eyelids close I see thy form,
Pure as the snow-drop, yet in blushes warm.
But oh! what followed?—strange effect of fright,
I dreamed that in my bed thou pass't the night . . .

Come, with thy innocence, thy smiles impart
Fresh joy to me, and mend each wicked heart,
Talk much of charity, and Love, too, teach:
'Tis mine to suffer, but 'tis thine to preach.

CHAPTER VIII

Knole at the End of the Eighteenth Century

JOHN FREDERICK SACKVILLE
3rd
Duke *of* Dorset

§ i

THE portrait by Gainsborough in the ball-room is of a man with a curved mouth, deep grey eyes, and powdered hair brushed back off his forehead. He looks out from the oval of his framing, beautiful and melancholy. " I have always looked on him as the most dangerous of men," said the Duchess of Devonshire, " for with that beauty of his he is so unaffected, and has a simplicity and a persuasion in his manner that makes one account very easily for the number of women he has had in love with him." There is much in him which recalls his forefather, Charles, the Dorset of the Restoration, but this is a personality less opulent, less voluminous, more wistful and more romantic; all his accessories are essentially of the eighteenth century—his Chinese page, his diamonds, his scarf-pin, his Italian mistress who caused so much scandal by dancing at the Opera in Paris with his Garter bound about her forehead. He is the immediate precursor of the generation which replaced by Gothic the Tudor windows in the Orangery, made serpentine some of the straight paths in the garden, and decorated the windows in the Colonnade with representations of knights in full armour. He himself escaped the baronial tendencies. He belonged to an age more delicate, more exquisite; an age of quizzing glasses, of flowered waistcoats, of buckled shoes, and of slim bejewelled swords. When he had his mistress sculpted, it was lying full-length on a couch, naked save for a single rose looping up her hair. When he had her drawn, it was pointing her little foot in the first step of a dance, a tambourine in her hand, and the Chinese boy in the background. When he wrote to his friends, it was in a bored, nonchalant style, half in English and half in French. His manner was " soft, quiet, and ingratiating." He treated the women who loved him with an easy heartlessness which failed to diminish their affection. He was possessed of no very great talents but those calculated to render life agreeable to him in the circles into which he was born, for it was his good fortune to be born handsome, rich, charming, and a duke, in a century when those qualifications were a certain passport to success.

John Frederick Sackville became Duke of Dorset at the age of twenty-four. He was the son of that Lord John Sackville who passes across the annals of the family early in life as a poet and cricketer, and later as a sad and shabby figure, "always dirtily clad," living under mild restraint at Vevey, a victim to melancholia. There was, however, no hint as yet of this hereditary strangeness of temper in his son, the new Duke of Dorset. The young man came brilliantly into his new possessions, paid the undertaker £66 6s. for the late duke's funeral, paid the Sheriff £418 2s. for "things taken at Knole" —from which it would seem that the late duke had died in debt—bought four thousand ounces of silver, and entertained his neighbours and tenantry to a feast in celebration of his succession, at which sixty stone of beef, mutton, and veal were consumed, thirty-four pounds of wax-lights used, and musicians provided. It is curious to see how the price of wine had altered between the days of Charles II and this time ; namely, 1769. Claret now cost 54*s*. a dozen, Burgundy 60*s*. a dozen, Champagne 97*s*. a dozen, and port for the servants' table cost 20*s*. a dozen, in comparison with the few shillings paid per gallon a century earlier. The only thing which did not [*see* p. 133] alter in proportion is beer, for which 35*s*. a hogshead was paid in the seventeenth century and £2 10*s*. a hogshead in the eighteenth. The young duke's time, we are told, was " devoted to gallantry and pleasure among the fashionable circles as well in France and Italy as in England," a phrase which begins to acquire a fatally familiar ring through the generations of the family. Perhaps nothing else could reasonably be expected of him. Life offered him too great an ease and too many advantages; why should he have rejected them ? Before he had been for a year in the enjoyment of his honours and estates he had set out on the Grand Tour accompanied by the celebrated Nancy Parsons and a train of singers, actors, and Bohemians, who clustered round him in every European capital which he visited. Echoes of his extravagance and his escapades come down to us from Paris and from Rome. He entertained lavishly every evening, inviting only those who could amuse his already blasé appetite; he rescued his Nancy Parsons in the nick of time as she was about to be abducted from a masked ball by a noble Venetian; he indulged his taste for the fine arts " even beyond the limits of his fortune "; he bought a Perugino, he bought a doubtful Titian, and a number of Italian primitives; he bought from a Mr. Jenkins in Rome " *the figure of Demosthenes in the act of delivering an oration*, a fine Grecian relick in marble," and a

178

bronze cast of the Gladiator Repellens, on whose shield he caused his own coat-of-arms to be embossed. This kind of existence he continued to lead for two or three years, when he threw over Nancy Parsons, returned to England, and became the lover of a Mrs. Elizabeth Armistead. Meanwhile, it appears from his account-books that large sums were being spent by his orders on both outdoor and indoor repairs at Knole. He put down new floors, altered some of the windows, and bought further enormous quantities of silver, 5920 ounces in one year alone, costing £2463 17s. 7d., and including a hundred and forty-four silver plates, eight dozen each of forks and spoons, dishes of all kinds, covers, and tureens. Occupied with Knole, love affairs, and cricket, he dawdled away a particularly gilded youth. Details from his account-books give a good idea of his expenses and occupations:

	£	s.	d.
Mrs. Gardiner, lace ruffles	41	0	0
Butler, new chain	80	0	0
Opera, expenses last winter	17	19	0
Opera, subscription	21	0	0
Paid Sir Joshua Reynolds	78	15	0

Mrs. Elizabeth Armistead reigned for three years, but the duke had other diversions in other circles: the gay, frivolous, and wanton Lady Betty Hamilton, trailing from ball to ball with her suitors in her wake, set her heart upon him, and he, not unresponsive, was ready to trifle so long as he was not expected to marry. Lady Betty was finally married off to Lord Derby, reputed the ugliest and the richest peer in England.

Many were the means employed till Lord Derby's constant and assiduous care veiled the ugliness of his person before the idol he worshipped. Time and despair made Lady Betty give a hasty and undigested consent. After a day of persecutions from every quarter, while a hair-dresser was adorning her unhappy head, she traced the consent with a pencil on a scrap of paper, and sent it wet with her tears to her mother.

A re-shuffle now took place: the duke became the new Lady Derby's lover, and Lord Derby became the lover of Mrs. Armistead. This arrangement, however, was not of long duration. Lord Derby fell in love with Elizabeth Farren; Lady Derby, it was rumoured, ran away and had to be brought back by her brother, the Duke of Hamilton: still bent upon marrying the Duke of Dorset, she wished to divorce Lord Derby, but was foiled by the prudence of Miss Farren. The gossips of London were much excited by all these occurrences. Lady Sarah Lennox wrote: "It is no scandal to tell you it is imagined that the Duke of Dorset will marry Lady Derby. I am told she has been and still is most thoroughly attached to him." It would be satisfactory to know exactly what part Dorset played; I fear not a very creditable one. Lady Derby was an impulsive, headstrong, attractive creature, capable of real passion under all her lightheartedness and easy virtue; her husband was unfaithful to her; her rival more sage and experienced than she herself; her lover ready to take what he could without incurring an irksome responsibility. My grandfather's sister, Lady Derby, used to show at Knowsley the window through which the Duke of Dorset was reported to have been admitted to the house, disguised as a gardener, and it was commonly supposed that the infant Lady Elizabeth Stanley was in reality the duke's daughter. But when the affair threatened to become too serious he was only too ready to resume his travels abroad.

I can only suppose that it was during one of his

absences that Horace Walpole went to Knole and found it not at all to his liking, for he draws a picture of the place in a state of desertion which would surely not have been warranted had the duke and his household been in occupation:

I came to Knole [*he writes to Lady Ossory*], and that was a medley of various feelings ! Elizabeth and Burleigh and Buckhurst ; and then Charles [*he means Richard*] and Anne, Dorset and Pembroke, and Sir Edward Sackville, and then a more engaging Dorset, and Villiers and Prior, and then the old duke and duchess, and Lady Betty Germaine, and the court of George II.

The place is stripped of its beeches and honours, and has neither beauty nor prospects. The house, extensive as it is, seemed dwindled to the front of a college, and has the silence and solitude of one. It wants the cohorts of retainers, and the bustling jollity of the old nobility, to disperse the gloom. I worship all its faded splendour, and enjoy its preservation, and could have wandered over it for hours with satisfaction, but there was such a heterogenous housekeeper as poisoned all my enthusiasm. She was more like one of Mrs. St. John's Abigails than an inhabitant of a venerable mansion, and shuffled about in slippers, and seemed to *admire* how I could care about the pictures of such old *frights* as covered the walls.

§ ii

I have said that cricket as well as love affairs occupied the duke's time, and in this he was only carrying on the tradition begun by his father and his uncle, who were both enthusiastic cricketers and took part in the first match recorded as having been played at Sevenoaks, in 1734, between Kent and Sussex, Lord John Sackville and Lord Middlesex playing, of course, for Kent. Six years later Sevenoaks played London on the famous Vine cricket ground at Sevenoaks—the first match recorded on the Vine. The young Duke of Dorset inherited his father's taste, keeping in his employ professional cricketers such as Bowra, Miller, and Minskull, and we have endless details of the matches played, an old print of one match taking place on the Vine between the duke's men and Sir Horace Mann's men, which shows the players all wearing jockey-caps and finally a number of cricketing ballads, more noticeable for their enthusiasm than for their excellence:

> *His Grace the Duke of Dorset came* [we read],
> *The next enrolled in skilful fame.*
> *Equalled by few, he plays with glee,*
> *Nor peevish seeks for victory,*
> *And far unlike the modern way*
> *Of blocking every ball at play,*
> *He firmly stands with bat upright*
> *And strikes with his athletic might,*
> *Sends forth the ball across the mead*
> *And scores six notches for the deed.*

There is in particular a great contest between Kent and Surrey, celebrated in a ballad of sixty-five verses, in which

> *The fieldsmen, stationed on the lawn,*
> *Well able to endure,*
> *Their loins with snow-white satin vests*
> *That day had guarded sure,*

and it is related that in this match also the Duke of Dorset was playing for the honour of his county, for we are told that

> *Young Dorset, like a baron bold,*
> *His jetty hair undrest,*
> *Ran foremost of the company,*
> *Clad in a milk-white vest.*

Despite the efforts of the duke and the men of Kent, they were defeated by Surrey, and the duke met with disaster:

> " *O heavy news !* " *the Rector cried,*
> " *The Vine can witness be,*
> *We have not any cricketer*
> *Of such account as he.*"

It is satisfactory to learn that in the return match Surrey was beaten.

§ iii

We come now to the period when " the gay Duke of Dorset became ambassador in Paris," and " his encouragement of the Parisian ballet was the amazement and envy of his age." It is entertaining, and rather sad, to read both his official despatches from Paris and his private letters to his friends, and to reflect that while he was writing to the Duchess of Devonshire, " I suppose you will hear talk of my ball, it has made a great noise at Paris"; or to the Foreign Office, "It is hardly possible to conceive a moment of more perfect tranquility than the present, the French government, free from the late causes of its anxiety, appears entirely bent upon improving the advantages of peace,"—it is sad, and certainly ironical, to reflect that the taking of the Bastille was distant by a paltry three years. With no foreboding of those tremendous events, which more than any war, more even than the career of Napoleón, were to change the fortunes of humanity, the Court of France and the English envoy continued on their course of enjoyment. The Duke of Dorset became, naturally, extremely popular in Paris. He was himself not sure that he wholly liked the French:

All the French are *aimable, si vous voulez*, but they are capricious and inconstant, especially the women [*he wrote home to the Duchess of Devonshire*]; in short, I have really no friend here but Mrs. B. [Marie Antoinette], and then I see her so seldom that I forget half what I want to say to her. The Frenchmen are all jealous and treacherous, so that between the capriciousness of the fair sex and the want of confidence I have in the other *je me sens vraiment malheureux*, I assure you, my dearest duchess.

But the French had no corresponding fault to find. The English ambassador was princely and lavish; he was spending money, as he himself owned, at the rate of £11,000 a year; he was greatly in the Queen's favour, so greatly that he has been included by certain authorities (notably Tilly) in their lists of her lovers. Sir Nathaniel Wraxall, who, although an inaccurate was yet a contemporary writer, says that this was not so, and that he has seen a letter-case, preserved by the duke, full of Marie Antoinette's notes addressed to him. Wraxall says that they were written on private concerns, commissions that she requested him to execute for her, principally regarding English articles of dress or ornament, and other innocent and unimportant matters. Whether Dorset was or was not her lover is not of the smallest importance; and surely no one would grudge, at this distance of time, any pleasure that a princess so young and so unfortunate might have enjoyed in life.

A question in which the Duke was naturally much interested was the affair of the diamond necklace. His despatches to the Foreign Office are full of references to the story, from August 1785 onwards:

The usually credited account is, that the Cardinal [de Rohan] has forged an order from the Queen to the Jeweller of the Crown to deliver to him diamonds to the amount of

1,600,000 livres, and which diamonds he actually received. What makes this event the more extraordinary is that the Cardinal is known to be a man of extremely good parts, and is in the enjoyment of the greatest honour and revenues to which any subject in the Church can aspire.

And again:

Mme. de la Motte, from an apprehension that her life is in danger, affects to have lost her senses. The jailer, upon entering her room the day before yesterday, was some time before he discovered her, and at length found her under her bed, quite naked.

It would, of course, take up too much space to give all Dorset's despatches on this subject. I mention them chiefly because a large proportion of the diamonds composing the original necklace are at Knole, one half having been purchased by the Duke of Dorset after the necklace had been split up and brought to England, and the other half by the Duke of Sutherland. This, at least, is the tradition; and there is some evidence to support it, in a receipt among the Knole papers:

Received of his Grace the DUKE of DORSET nine hundred and seventy-five pounds for a brilliant necklace.

£975   For MR. JEFFERYS and self, WM JONES.

and this receipt is endorsed " Paid 1790," which tallies with the date when the necklace was sold by De la Motte to Jefferys, a jeweller in Piccadilly. They are beautiful diamonds, small, but very blue, and are set at present in the shape of a tasselled diadem.

Another topic which temporarily exercised the duke while in Paris was the " very extraordinary proposal " made to the French Government by a M. Montgolfier to construct a balloon of a certain diameter to carry sixteen persons. The project [the despatch continues] is to carry on a trade between this part and the South of France ; Paris and Marseilles are the two places named. The balloon is to be freighted with plate glass, and the return to be made in reams of paper. M. de Calonne has hitherto received the proposal with great coolness, as M. Montgolfier requires an advance of 60,000 livres Tournais. It is, however, under contemplation, as M. Montgolfier has declared his intention of making the offer to our government in case he does not meet with encouragement here. It is said that the Comptroller General rather discourages enterprises of this sort, as any further progress in the art of conducting balloons might tend to prejudice the revenues of the City of Paris, which will shortly be surrounded by a wall, the cost of which is estimated at four or five millions.

The duke naturally thought M. Montgolfier's plans nonsensical:

I should almost scruple to mention to your Lordship an undertaking so extraordinary [*he says*] had I not heard from exceedingly good authority that such a plan is seriously in agitation. Great credit is given to M. Montgolfier's superior skill in these matters, and that gentleman's friends are sanguine in their expectations of his success. The weight he proposes to carry *exceeds that of a waggon-load !*

He gives some further details of what M. Montgolfier, who " pretends to have at last discovered means of directing the course of Balloons," proposes to do:

He has obtained the sanction of M. de Calonne for his first experiment, which is to be made the first day of next May, when he engages to depart from a town in Auvergne, distant from Paris 150 miles, and to descend at or near this City in the space of seven hours.

A month later he writes:

The government has at last accepted M. Montgolfier's proposal. 30,000 livres are to be granted to him in advance for the experiment, and if it succeeds the whole of his expenses will be paid without any examination of his accounts, a pension granted to him, and every honorary recompense bestowed on him to which he can aspire. He pretends to have discovered the means of guiding his machine, but it was not till after his project to England, in case of refusal here, that it was accepted.

On such topics as the diamond necklace and M. Montgolfier and current affairs Dorset beguiled his leisure and that of the Foreign Office. There is no indication that he detected any signs of the trouble in store. It is true that occasionally he writes in this strain:

Their Majesties, the Dauphin, and the rest of the Royal family, are removed from Fontainebleau to Versailles. The expenses attending these journeys of the Court is incredible. The duc de Polignac told me that he had given orders for 2115 horses for this service. . . . Besides this, an adequate proportion of horses are ordered for the removal of the heavy baggage. . . . It is asserted that M. de Calonne will be under the necessity of borrowing at least eight millions of livres next year,

and that after the fall of the Bastille he was moved to write: " I really think it necessary that some public caution be given to put those upon their guard who may propose to visit this part of the continent." But beyond these occasional comments he does not seem to have been troubled by any thoughts of the future. He did not foresee that his friend "Mrs. B.," to whom after his return to England he continued to supply English gloves, would lose upon the scaffold that little head which had carried so gaily the butterfly or the frigate, or that within two or three years' time the English newspapers would be writing: "The Duke of Dorset's seat at Knole is a place of rendezvous for the banished French *noblesse* at this time resident in England," or that he would be entertaining there as a fugitive his friend Champcenetz, a young officer in the Swiss Guards and author of a " *Petit traité de l'amour des femmes pour les sots.*" Dorset would no doubt have proved a perfectly adequate ambassador in normal times, but that vast situation with its infinite ramifications was beyond an intellect that accepted for granted the existing régime under which dukes were born for pleasure and labourers were not. But with all the foresight in the world it is difficult to see what he could have done, or how the course of history could have been affected, had he sent home grave warnings instead of babbling of the diamond necklace and M. Montgolfier.

There was another distraction for him in Paris: Giannetta Baccelli, an Italian dancer. The duke seems to have lost his head completely over her for the time being, for he gave her his Garter to wear as a hairribbon, with " HONI SOIT QUI MAL Y PENSE " in diamonds, brought her home to England with him, sent her to a ball in Sevenoaks wearing the family jewels—which provoked a great scandal in the county—and gave her one of the towers at Knole, which to this day remains, through the mispronunciation of the English servants, " Shelley's Tower." It was for this lady, or so the rumour ran, that he finally rejected the faithful and unfortunate Lady Derby. There was nothing that Dorset would not do for Baccelli. He had her painted by Reynolds, and painted and drawn by Gainsborough, and sculpted from the nude. He even wrote to his friend the Duchess of Devonshire asking her to do what she could for his protégée, " I don't ask you to do anything for her openly," he wrote, " but I hope *que quand il s'agit de ses talents* you will commend her. I assure you," he adds rather pathetically,

LADY BETTY GERMAIN'S BEDROOM

Geo. P.

The Three Children

GEORGE JOHN FREDERICK SACKVILLE, 4th Duke of Dorset

LADY MARY SACKVILLE,   LADY ELIZABETH SACKVII

From the portrait by John Hoppner, previously at Knole and now in the possession of Mr. Thomas
Lamont, New York

" she is *une bonne fille*, very clever, and *un excellent cœur*, and her dancing is really wonderful."

Gainsborough's large full-length portrait of Baccelli, originally at Knole, has been sold; but his pencil sketch for it remains, rather faded and very delicate of line. It is drawn in the ball-room: Baccelli stands on a model's throne, pointing her toe and lifting up her skirt; Gainsborough himself stands in front of her, a palette in his hand, so that he turns his back towards the person looking at the drawing; the Chinese page, in a round hat, stands by. It reconstructs with great vividness the scene of her posing in the ball-room. The only pity is that the artist should not have drawn in the duke, who was surely there, looking on, and criticizing and making suggestions. The receipt for the big picture is at Knole, though no mention is made of the drawing (*see illustration facing p.* 208):

Received of his Grace the DUKE of DORSET one hundred guineas in full for two ¾ portraits of his Grace, one full-length of Mad^sle Baccelli, two Landskips, and one sketch of a beggar boy and girl.

£105   THOMAS GAINSBOROUGH, *June* 15, 1784.

One of the " two ¾ portraits of his Grace "mentioned in this receipt is the one now in the ball-room, one of the most beautiful Gainsboroughs I know—included with five other pictures for the ludicrous sum of £105.

Reynolds' portrait of the dancer shows a mischievous and attractive face, with slightly slanting eyes, peeping out from behind a mask which she holds up in her hand. The duke even went to the length of ordering the portraits of the servants he had provided for her, and among the collection of servants' portraits in Black Boy Passage are Daniel Taylor and Elinor Law, servants of Mad^me Baccelli; Mrs. Edwards, attendant on Mad^me Baccelli; and Philip Louvaux, servant to Mad^me Baccelli. She evidently, with her servants and her tower, had a regular establishment at Knole, and many receipts bearing her signature witness the duke's generosity towards her: "Received 7th April 1786 of Mr. Burlington [the agent] the sum of fifty pounds on account of his Grace the Duke of Dorset, Jannette Baccelli," and so on. They had several children, all of whom died in babyhood, except one, alluded to in the following letter: "The duke has a very fine boy to whom Baccelli is mother, now at school near Knole. This, we think, is the only surviving progeny of the alliance," but, much as I should like to know, I have no idea what became of this romantically-begotten scion, or even of whether he lived to grow up.

Perhaps the "heterogenous housekeeper" of Horace Walpole's letter was Baccelli's importation, for in another place he writes disgustedly of "Knole, which disappointed me much. But unless you know how vast and venerable I thought I remembered it, I cannot give you the measure of my surprise; but then there was a trapes of a housekeeper, who, I suppose, was the Baccelli's dresser, and who put me out of humour . . ."

The connection seems to have lasted for a long time, for it is not until the end of 1789 that we come across an old newspaper cutting announcing with curious candour that "the Duke of Dorset and the Baccelli have just separated, and she is said to have behaved very well," so that she eclipsed the records of Nancy Parsons, of Mrs. Elizabeth Armistead, and of poor Lady Derby. It is, I think, a not unpicturesque incident in the story of Knole—the dancer sitting in those stately rooms to Reynolds and Gainsborough, or descending from her tower to walk in the garden with the duke, attended by the Chinese boy carrying her gloves, her fan, or her parasol. Those were the days when the Clock Tower, oddly recalling a pagoda, was but newly erected; when the great rose-and-gold Chinese screen in the Poets' Parlour was new and brilliant in the sun; when the Coromandel chests were new toys; and the Italian pictures and the statuary brought back by the duke from Rome were still pointed out as the latest acquisitions. And no doubt then the statue of the Baccelli reposing in her lovely nudity on her couch was not relegated to the attic, where a subsequent and more prudish generation sent it, but stood somewhere in the living-rooms, where it might be seen and admired in the presence of the smiling model. Amusement was caused too, no doubt, among the guests of the duke and the dancer by Sir Joshua's portrait of the Chinese boy squatting on his heels, a fan in his hand, and the square toes of his red shoes protruding from beneath his robes. It was more original to have a Chinese page than to have a black one; everybody had a black one: "Dear Mama," wrote the Duchess of Devonshire to her mother, " George Hanger has sent me a Black boy, eleven years old and very honest, but the duke don't like me having a black, and yet I cannot bear the poor wretch being ill-used; if you liked him instead of Michel I will send him, he will be a cheap servant and you will make a Christian of him and a good boy; if you don't like him they say Lady Rockingham wants one." But the black page at Knole, of which there had always been one since the days of Lady Anne Clifford, and who had always been called John Morocco regardless of what his true name might be, had been replaced by a Chinaman ever since the house steward had killed the John Morocco of the moment in a fight in Black Boy's Passage. This particular Chinese boy whom I have mentioned, whose real name was Hwang-a-Tung, but whom the English servants, much as they called Baccelli Madam Shelley, more conveniently renamed Warnoton—fell on fortunate days when he came to Knole, for not only was he painted by Sir Joshua, but he was educated at the duke's expense at the Grammar School in Sevenoaks.

§ iv

The year after the parting in which the Baccelli was reported to have behaved so well, the duke married. His bride was an heiress, Arabella Diana Cope, who brought the duke, according to his own statement, a dowry of £140,000. She must have been an imposing figure, if one may trust Hoppner's portrait, which shows her walking in a white muslin dress, a little dog frisking round her feet, and tall feathers on her head; and Wraxall, who certainly knew her, says, with the touch of awe and even dislike perceptible between the lines of all his accounts of her, that " her person, though not feminine, might then be denominated handsome; and, if her mind was not highly cultivated or refined, she could boast of intellectual endowments that fitted her for the active business of life." Wraxall writes, possibly, with a prejudiced pen, for at one time he was employed in sorting and classifying the Knole manuscripts, and in this matter his views clashed with those of her Grace and her Grace's second husband; the business was abandoned half way through, but Wraxall's trace remains in the neat, ejaculatory notes which I find on the reverse side of many of the papers—

" curious ! " or " not without merit ! " This may account for the subtle spitefulness of his remarks. Nevertheless, I imagine that Knole perceived under the duchess' régime a considerable contrast with the days of the merry and pleasure-loving Baccelli. The new duchess was a severe and orderly lady, " under the dominion of no passion except the love of money, her taste for power and pleasure always subordinate to her economy," and the duke himself, perhaps under the influence of his wife, began to turn from his extravagant ways towards parsimony, curtailing his expenses in spite of the enormous increase in his income, and becoming, moreover, irascible, fretful, morbid, and quarrelsome. The days of his patronage of opera and Parisian ballet were over, the days when he was confident that the talk of his ball in Paris would reach the ears of the Duchess of Devonshire in London. His expenses at Knole were reported to be reduced to four or five thousand a year, yet he could not endure to hear the praise of other houses, for Knole he considered "as possessing everything." It is not an attractive picture of the gay duke's declining years. Hoppner, who had been staying at Knole for nine or ten days painting the three children, described the duke as most unpleasant in his temper, anxious and saving, humoursome and uncomfortable, " not suffering the dinner to be all placed on the table," and when, playing at Casino, he lost fifteen shillings to Hoppner he "fretted when the cards he wished for were taken up." The three children were brought up with the utmost severity; they were scarcely allowed to speak in the presence of their elders; and little Lord Middlesex was sent out of the room in disgrace at luncheon for asking his sister for the salt. Yet I fancy that the real control, under a show of submission, was exercised by that commanding figure, the duchess. She never betrayed a. .y signs of exasperation, whether the duke sent away the dinner, or grumbled that Neckar was a man of no family, or that Mr. Hailes, the secretary, was a man of no family either—much to Mr. Hailes' discomposure. This dwelling upon family was one of his many crotchets, and he was fond of pointing out that the Sackvilles had never branched, but remained the only family of that name in the Kingdom, and would draw attention to the coincidence that Sackville Street was the longest street in London without branch or turning. Prudent and long-suffering, no doubt the duchess had in her mind the advantages she intended to secure when she should be no longer a wife and sick-nurse, but a widow. Baccelli's statue was in the attic, and Mr. Ozias Humphrey, of the Royal Academy, was quite out of favour because he went to Knole in the duke's absence and took possession of a room without previously showing proper attention to the duchess. She presided calmly, while the duke fretted and economized, and quarrelled with his friends, and deteriorated in intellect, and became a prey to gloom, and grew old and sad before his time; she presided unruffled, for all the while she rested satisfied in her knowledge of his testamentary dispositions. He was, in fact, although only in the fifties, already a very ill man. He was falling rapidly into a deeper and deeper melancholy, and there is a tradition that towards the end he could only be soothed by the playing of two musicians in a neighbouring room—the room now called the Music Room, in which hang, rather ironically, Reynolds' portrait of the Baccelli peeping out from behind her mask, and Vigée Lebrun's portrait of the grave, grey-

haired lady, Arabella Diana, Duchess of Dorset. He
sat in the library, his hands fumbling at the breast-pin
in his *jabot*, while the soothing strains reached him,
veiled by distance. Veiled by distance, too, the
memories of his past floated to him on the music, and
melted with the music into the solace of a confused and
wistful harmony. The past, so luminous, was not
wholly lost, since in memory it was still recoverable.
There had been the fun of the masked ball in Rome;
there had been the clandestine hours of tenderness
with Betty Hamilton; there had been Versailles;
there had been the days when he could glance down
through the window and see Baccelli flirting with Sir
Joshua on the lawn. The musicians in the neighbouring room played on. He had been twenty-four when
Knole had come to him; he had not had to wait for
his good things until he was grown too sober to enjoy
them. It had been so easy to accept the urbanity, the
empressement, everyone was eager to lavish; so pleasant
to move in a world so bland, so obliging, and so polite.
No effort had been necessary; the fat quails had
dropped ready roasted into his mouth. No effort: a
smile there; a gracious word here; tossed alike with a
casual, if good-humoured, contempt. Surveying himself in his mirror while his valet knelt to buckle the
diamond Order round his knee, flicking with a lace
pocket-handkerchief at a few grains of powder fallen
upon his coat, he had been secure in the safe conduct
of his great name and his personal charm. And if the
faint ghosts whispered round him now in the quiet
library at Knole—a fair head thrust at him upon a pike,
the reproachful eyes of Lady Derby, the stilled limbs
of those half-Italian babies that the Baccelli had borne
him—why, he could banish them: Lord Middlesex slept

in his nursery upstairs, and the tall duchess watched, effaced though vigilant, from a corner of the library. But when she rose and came towards him, thinking that he had fallen asleep in his nodding over the fire, he repulsed her fretfully, with the gesture of an old man, and wondered at himself in his confused and unhappy mind for this anomalous discourtesy towards a woman.

Next door to the Music Room hangs the lovely full-length of the three children, painted by Hoppner while on that uncomfortable visit. One is bound to admit that their appearance bears no impress of the grand, solemn, and gloomy household in which they were being brought up. The little boy, rosy, flaxen-curled, in high nankeen trousers and a soft frilly shirt, has his arms round his baby sister, who, with bare toes, is looking sulkily at her elder sister's shoes; they are out in the park; nothing could be more natural or unconstrained. My grandfather used to show me the baby girl, telling me that while Hoppner was seeking for a pose for his picture a grievance arose between the two little girls because one had shoes and the other had not, and that on Lord Middlesex taking his sister into his arms for consolation, Hoppner rushed at them exclaiming that he could not improve upon the charm of this accidental pose. I think this story has a convincing ring about it. Certainly it was the only anecdote which my grandfather had to tell of any picture in the house; usually he did not know a Hoppner from a Vandyck, a Kneller from a Gainsborough. He said that he had the story straight from his mother, Lady Elizabeth, the sulky baby of Hoppner's picture, and the young woman in fancy dress of Beechey's portrait in the same room.

The only pleasant aspect of these later years of the

gay duke's life is his friendship and constant employment of the artists of his day. Before he fell into what Wraxall calls his " mental alienation " he counted Reynolds among his intimates, was a pall-bearer at his funeral in Westminster Abbey, and accumulated so many works of that artist at Knole, including one at the back of which is written, " Sir Joshua Reynolds, painted by himself and presented to his Grace the Duke of Dorset in 1780," that what was once the Crimson Drawing-Room became known as the Reynolds Room; and the Reynolds Room it is to this day. Madame Vigée Lebrun stayed at Knole, which she found too gloomy for her taste, the duchess warning her, the first time they sat down to dinner, " You will find it very dull, for we never speak at table." Ozias Humphrey, before he was so unfortunate as to offend the duchess, contributed a number of canvases to the duke's collection:

Two pastels, 12 guineas each.

KNIGHTSBRIDGE, *June* 25*th*, 1792.

	£	s.	d.
His Grace the Duke of Dorset to Ozias Humphrey, for a portrait in miniature	16	16	0
A small crayon picture of the crossing-sweeper at Hyde Park Corner with a rich gold frame and glass	21	0	0
A portrait of the Duchess of Dorset in crayons	12	12	0
	£50	8	0

Received of his Grace the Duke of DORSET the sum of fifty pounds in full for the amount of the annexed bill.

OZIAS HUMPHREY.

It is perhaps significant of his new economy that the duke ignored the eight shillings.

With Opie, too, he was on friendly terms, and

amongst the other receipts at Knole is one from Opie for the portrait of Edmund Burke for £24 3s. There is also a letter at Knole from Burke, who probably knew his Grace's weakness for his house:

My Lord,   Duke St., *Sept.* 14, 1791.

I am just now honoured with your Grace's letter, and am extremely concerned that it is not in my power to accept your Grace's most obliging invitation. I have great respect for its present possessor ; and as for the place, I, who am something of a lover of all antiquities, must be a very great admirer of Knole. I think it the most interesting thing in England. It is pleasant to have preserved in one place the succession of the several tastes of ages ; a pleasant habitation for the time, a grand repository of whatever has been pleasant at all times. This is not the sort of place which every banker, contractor, or Nabob can create at his pleasure. . . . I would not change Knole if I were the Duke of Dorset for all the foppish structures of this age.

Other receipts at Knole make it clear that the average price for a half-length was £37, while for a full-length by Reynolds the duke paid £300.

There is also a mention in a contemporary diary that the duke asked Hoppner for his portrait, which he promised should be hung next to Sir Joshua's portrait of himself. The diary notes that Ozias Humphrey's *Selbstbildnis* is " still in the room, but has been removed from its place next the Reynolds." It is " still in the room " now, a man with a delicate face and a pointed nose, on the wall with Gainsborough's *Lord George Sackville*, Sir Joshua's *Samuel Foote*, his *Oliver Goldsmith*, his *Peg Woffington*, and his own portrait; but the Hoppner for which the duke asked is not there, and never was; no doubt Hoppner was not sufficiently encouraged by the uncomfortable visit to send so valuable an acknowledgment.

At this period England lay under the fear of an invasion by the young victorious Bonaparte, and a scheme was set on foot for raising a corps of infantry to be called the Knole volunteers; I recently came across some of their accoutrements in an old locker at Knole; they had an amateurish look. A document bearing many blots and the signatures of all the volunteers—or, in some cases, their mark—is also at Knole:

HIS GRACE *the* DUKE *of* DORSET's offer of raising a Corps of Infantry, to consist of Sixty Men, to be called the *Knole Volunteers*, for the purpose of preserving Order and protecting property in the Parish and Neighbourhood of Sevenoaks having been accepted, and George Stone, Stephen Woodgate, and Thomas Mortimer Kelson being appointed officers by his Majesty to command the same, they propose the following Rules and Regulations, which they hope will be cheerfully submitted to by all who have voluntarily come forward to offer their services in the said Corps at this important Crisis :

1st.   *That* each individual attend twice a week for the purpose of exercising from half after Six o'clock to half after Eight o'clock in the Evening.

2nd.   As a regular attendance is particularly essential, it is proposed that the small Sum of Sixpence be paid by every person not present to answer to his Name when called over at the time appointed, unless it appears he is prevented by Sickness, which forfeits, should there be any, shall be spent by the Corps at the end of the year in any manner they shall think proper.

3rd.   That every Man appears clean and properly accoutered.

4thly. That they do their utmost Endeavour to learn their Exercise, paying proper respect to their Officers.

Finally, they wish it to be clearly understood that their Services shall not be required to extend further than the

Parish and Neighbourhood of Sevenoaks, unless it be for the purpose of guarding Prisoners or Convoys as far as one Stage.   KNOLE, 22 *May* 1798.

But it is improbable that the duke had much to do with the raising or organisation of this corps, for during the last twenty months of his life his irascibility turned to definite melancholia, and he remained at Knole more or less alone with the duchess keeping a jealous guard over him. It is impossible not to draw the parallel between his end and that of Charles the Restoration earl, his great-grandfather, remembering especially the wildness and extravagance in which both had spent their youth; but whereas Charles was carried away to Bath at the end by that sordid woman Ann Roche, the duke was carefully tended in his own great house by the reserved and prudent woman he had married, too dignified to be accused save under the veil of polite phrases of intriguing to get the control of his affairs into her own hands. So he sank gradually, and in 1799, at the age of fifty-four, he died, when it was found that he had so disposed of his lands, his fortune, and his boroughs that Arabella Diana was left with so great an accumulation of wealth and of parliamentary influence as had " scarcely ever vested, among us, in a female, and a widow."

CHAPTER IX

Knole in the Nineteenth Century

§ i

THE new Duke of Dorset was only five years old when his father's dignities descended so prematurely on to his small yellow head, but he had a capable mentor in the person of his mother, and before two years had elapsed her authority was reinforced by that of a stepfather. This was Lord Whitworth, recently Ambassador to the Courts of Catherine II. and Paul I. The circumstances of Lord Whitworth's recall had been in the least degree mysterious. Various rumours were current; amongst others, that he had offended the Czar in the following somewhat ludicrous manner: the Czar having forbidden that any empty carriage should pass before a certain part of his palace, Lord Whitworth, uninformed of the regulation, ordered his coach to meet him at a point which would entail passing over the forbidden area. The sentry held up the coach; the servants persisted in driving on; they came to blows; and the Czar, when the affair came to his ears, ordered Lord Whitworth's servants to be beaten, the horses to be beaten, and the coach to be beaten too. Lord Whitworth, in a fit of rage and petulance, dismissed his servants, ordered the horses to be shot, and the coach to be broken into pieces and thrown into the Neva.

He appears to have had at least one trait in common with the Sackvilles themselves, at any rate in early life, for it was said of him that he was " more distinguished during this period of his career by success in gallantries than by any professional merits or brilliant services."

Even at the time of his marriage, when, returning from Russia to England, he found available the wealthy and desirable relict of his friend the late Dorset, he was heavily entangled with a lady named Countess Gerbetzow, whose partiality for the English Ambassador had been such that she had placed her own fortune at his disposal for the purpose of clothing himself and defraying the expenses of his household. In return for this affection and assistance Lord Whitworth promised her marriage as soon as she could divorce her husband; but during the course of the divorce proceedings the Ambassador was recalled, and left for England on the understanding that Countess Gerbetzow would follow him there as soon as she conveniently could. Meanwhile he made the acquaintance of the more eligible duchess, became engaged to her, and lost no time in marrying her. Countess Gerbetzow had, however, by now obtained her divorce, and was travelling across Europe on her way to England: at Leipzic she learnt from a newspaper that Lord Whitworth in London was engaged to the Duchess of Dorset. Indignant and outraged, she flew post-haste to London. Too late: she arrived only to find that the marriage had already been celebrated. But she would not allow the matter to rest there, and "her reclamations, which were of too delicate and serious a nature to be despised, at length compelled the duchess, most reluctantly, to pay her Muscovite rival no less a sum than ten thousand pounds." Whether the duchess continued to think Lord Whitworth worth the price is not recorded. If he was an expensive husband, he was certainly from the worldly standpoint a very successful one, and that was a standpoint the duchess was not likely to despise. He became successively Ambassador to the French Republic,

Lord Lieutenant of Ireland, and an earl, but " we may nevertheless be allowed to doubt," observes Wraxall, who claims Lord Whitworth's personal friendship,

whether a humbler matrimonial alliance might not have been attended with more felicity . . . united to a woman of inferior fortune and condition . . . he would certainly have presented an object of more rational envy and respect than as the second husband of a duchess, elevated by her connections to dignities and offices, subsisting on her possessions, and who will probably ere long inter him with an earl's coronet on his coffin.—I return [*says Wraxall, having thus dismissed the pair*] to Marie Antoinette.

I doubt whether the little duke was allowed a very exuberant enjoyment of his boyhood with this couple in authority over him. Children were strictly brought up in that generation, and it is clear that the duchess was by nature a severe and not very sympathetic woman. The little boy and his sisters must have been docile and well behaved in the great house and gardens which belonged to him in name only, but which in practice were entirely under his mother's control, for her to alter the windows as she pleased, and to put Lord Whitworth's cognizance in the stained glass beside the Sackville arms. I visualize—I scarcely know why—the duchess and Lord Whitworth almost as the jailers of the small inheritor. There is nothing to justify such a theory; and, indeed, very little record remains of that short life: there is his rocking-horse— an angular, long-necked, maneless animal, which in due course became my property, after passing through the two intervening generations—his brief friendship with Byron as a schoolboy, and his portrait as a tall, fair young man in dark blue academical robes. There is very little else to mark his passage across the stage of Knole.

He came, late in time, of a race never remarkable for strength of character, and the obituary notice which described him as having possessed gentle and engaging manners, tinctured by shyness, and of amiable temper, probably came nearer to the truth than the generality of such eulogies. Byron has told us nothing in the least illuminating of his friend. He has left a long address in verse, included in *Hours of Idleness*, in which he is careful to explain that the duke was his fag at Harrow,

> *Whom still affection taught me to defend,*
> *And made me less a tyrant than a friend,*
> *Though the harsh custom of our youthful band*
> *Bade thee obey, and gave me to command,*

and equally careful to remind him that they might in later years meet in the House of Lords,

> *Since chance has thrown us in the self-same sphere,*
> *Since the same senate, nay, the same debate,*
> *May one day claim our suffrage for the state.*

The rest of the poem is an exhortation to the duke, whose " passive tutors, fearful to dispraise," may

> *View ducal errors with indulgent eyes,*
> *And wink at faults they tremble to chastise,*

to be worthy of the record his ancestors have left him; of he who "called, proud boast! the British drama forth," and of that other one, Charles, "The pride of princes, and the boast of song"—to become, in fine, "Not Fortune's minion, but her noblest son." One suspects, in fact, that Byron himself viewed the errors of his ducal fag with an indulgent eye, and the depth of the friendship, on Byron's part at least, is easily measured by the letters he wrote on hearing of the duke's death—letters whose cynicism is perhaps atoned for by their frankness:

I have just been—or, rather, ought to be—very much shocked by the death of the Duke of Dorset [*he wrote to*

Tom Moore]. We were at school together, and then I was passionately attached to him. Since, we have never met—but once, I think, in 1805—and it would be a paltry affectation to pretend that I had any feeling for him worth the name. But there was a time in my life when this event would have broken my heart; and all I can say for it now is that—it is not worth breaking.

Adieu—it is all a farce.

And he alludes to it once more, a fortnight later, again writing to Moore, to say that " the death of poor Dorset—and the recollection of what I once felt, and ought to have felt now, but could not," has set him pondering.

That, then, is all which the boy could leave behind him—that he should set Byron, for a moment, pondering. From such slight traces—the English little boy of the Hoppner, the old-fashioned rocking-horse, and the portrait of the fair young man—we have to reconstruct as best we can an entire personality. We have to figure him running about the garden at Knole; kissing his mother's hand—surely never throwing his arms about her—his grave little bow to Lord Whitworth; the " your Grace " of his nurse's behests; the brief contact with the dazzling personality of Byron at Harrow; the stir with which he cannot have failed to anticipate the advantages of his life and his emancipation. We have the account of him playing tennis, when a ball hit him in the eye, and obliged him to be for ever after " continually applying leeches and blisters and ointments and other disagreeable remedies," and to be " very moderate in all exercises that heat or agitate the frame." We have, finally, his tragic end at the age of twenty-one, to which additional poignancy is lent by the fact that he had recently become engaged.

He had gone to Ireland, where his stepfather was

then Viceroy, to stay with his friend and quondam school-fellow Lord Powerscourt. On the day after his arrival the two young men, with Lord Powerscourt's brother, Mr. Wingfield, went out hunting, and after a fruitless morning they were about to return home when they put up a hare:

The hare made for the inclosures on Kilkenny Hill. They had gone but a short distance, when the Duke, who was an excellent forward horseman, rode at a wall, which was in fact a more dangerous obstacle than it appeared to be. . . . The Duke's mare attempted to cover all at one spring, and cleared the wall, but, alighting among the stones on the other side, threw herself headlong, and, turning in the air, came with great violence upon her rider, who had not lost his seat ; he undermost, with his back on one of the large stones, and she crushing him with all her weight on his chest, and struggling with all her might to recover her legs. The mare at length disentangled herself and galloped away. The Duke sprang upon his feet, and attempted to follow her, but soon found himself unable to stand, and fell into the arms of Mr. Farrel, who had run to his succour, and to whose house he was conveyed. Lord Powerscourt, in the utmost anxiety and alarm, rode full speed for medical assistance, leaving his brother, Mr. Wingfield, to pay every possible attention to the Duke. But, unfortunately, the injury was too severe to be counteracted by human skill ; life was extinct before any surgeon arrived. Such was the melancholy catastrophe that caused the untimely death of this young nobleman. He had been of age only three months, and had not taken his seat in the House of Lords [1815].

The author of this obituary notice was at great pains to clear the young man of any charge of " unseasonable levity ":

It has been said [*he observes*] that the Duke, in his dying moments, made use of the expression " I am off." He did so ; but not, as has been very erroneously supposed, by way of heroic bravado, or in a temper of unseasonable levity ; but

simply to signify to his attendants, who, in pulling off his
boots, had drawn him too forward on the mattress, and
jogged one of the chairs out of its place, that he was *slipping
off*, and wanted their aid to help him up into his former
position. He was the last person in the world to be guilty
of anything like levity upon any solemn occasion, much
less in his dying moments. The fact was, when he used
the expression " I am off " he had become very faint and
weak, and was glad to save himself the trouble of further
utterance. . . .

Now suppose a stranger to the real character of this
excellent youth to have heard no more of him than what he
would be most likely to hear of one whose constitutional
modesty concealed his virtues, namely, that he was very fond
of cricket, that he hurt his eye with a tennis-ball, that he
lost his life hunting, that his last words were " I am off " ;
would not a person possessed of this information, and no
more, naturally conclude that the Duke was a young man
of trivial mind, addicted to idle games and field sports, and
apt to make light of serious things ? How false a notion
would such a person form of the late Duke of Dorset ! As
to the four circumstances above alluded to, if he was fond of
cricket, it was in the evening generally that he played. When
he hurt his eye [it was on the 7th of December] he had been
at his books all the morning, and went between dinner and
dusk to take one set at tennis. When he lost his life hunting,
he had not hunted ten times the whole season. And what
have been represented as his last words were not his last
words ; and, even if they were, they had no other meaning
than " Pray prevent a helpless man from slipping down out
of his place." That he was not a mere sportsman, a mere
idler, or a mere trifler, witness the wet eyes that streamed at
every window in the streets of Dublin as his hearse was
passing by ; witness the train of carriages that composed his
funeral procession ; witness the throng of Nobility and
Gentlemen that attended his remains to the sea-shore ;
witness the families he had visited in Ireland ; witness the
reception of his corpse in England ; witness the amazing
concourse of friends, tenantry, and neighbours, that came
to hear the last rites performed, and to see him deposited in

the tomb ; witness the more endeared set of persons who
still mean to hover round the vault where he is laid !

§ ii

It now became apparent how exceedingly wise had
been the precautionary measures taken by the duchess
in regard to her husband's will. A distant cousin, the
son of Lord George, succeeded to the title as fifth and
last duke—this part of the succession was beyond the
reach of her control—but under the terms of the will
Knole became her property for life, and she received in
addition, on the death of her son, an increase in her
income of nine thousand a year. She must certainly
have been one of the richest women in England. Lord
Whitworth, meanwhile (till 1817), continued as Lord
Lieutenant of Ireland, and as the originals of the
following letters written to him by Sir Robert Peel,
with enclosures in Peel's handwriting, are at Knole,
I think it not wholly irrelevant to print them here, with
a few other notes, in view of their interest as being
written immediately after the battle of Waterloo, and
having, so far as I know, never before been published.

Private   IRISH OFFICE.
DEAR LORD WHITWORTH,   *June 22nd*, 1815.

YOU will receive by this express the official accounts
of the most desperate and most important action
in which the British arms have ever been engaged.
The Gazette details all the leading particulars—I have
just been at the War and Foreign Offices to collect any
further information that may be interesting to you. It is
evident that the attack was in a great degree a surprise upon
the Allies, Bonaparte collected his troops and advanced
with much greater rapidity than could have been expected.
It was supposed that it would have required three days to

bring the British force into line for a general engagement— but the suddenness of the attack gave them a much shorter time for preparation. It is said that on the 16th the Prussians lost fourteen thousand men.

All the private accounts attribute the success of the day to the Duke of Wellington's personal courage and extraordinary exertions. Flint will send you some interesting particulars on this point.

When the French Cavalry charged—the Duke placed himself in the centre of the square of infantry—a barrier that was impenetrable. Nothing could exceed the desperation with which the Cuirassiers fought. When they found they could make no impression on the solid mass of infantry —they halted in front and deliberately charged their pistols and shot at individuals of course without a chance of surviving. Lord Bathurst showed me a letter which he had received from Apsley. He says that Bonaparte had a scaffolding erected out of cannon shot from the top of which he saw the field of battle and the progress of the fight. When he found that success was almost hopeless he put himself at the head of the Imperial Guard—and charged in person. They were met by the first foot guards who overthrew them completely. The conduct of all the British infantry was beyond praise—Lord Wellington had about sixty-five thousand men in the field. Castlereagh told me that he thought Bonaparte must have lost the fourth of his army. This is of course mere conjecture.

Of the Regiments of Cavalry which distinguished themselves the Life Guards, the 10th, and the 18th are particularly mentioned. The field of battle after the action presented a most extraordinary sight. The panic of the French army after their failure—and the fruitlessness of the desperate courage they had shewn—was very great when the attack on our part commenced. They threw away their arms —knapsacks, etc., etc., in the greatest confusion. The Prussians gave no quarter in the pursuit.

The Duke and Blucher met for a moment after the action —in the village of *La heureuse Alliance* [sic].

The Belgian Cavalry and some of the British did not much distinguish themselves. I hear that the 7th, Lord Uxbridge's

own regiment, have not added much to their reputation—
but do not quote me for this piece of intelligence. General
Picton was shot through the head. He behaved with the
greatest possible gallantry.

Schartzenburg [sic] is supposed to have crossed the Rhine
with an immense force—perhaps 200,000 men on or about
the 20th. I should rather say it was expected that he would
cross about that time. There is no account from Paris—or
from the French army.

I have sent you a strange mixture of detached and un-
connected particulars. I heard them one by one—in such a
hurry—and am now obliged to write to you in such a hurry
that I may not detain the express that I cannot reduce them
into any shape.

The consequence of our success must infallibly lead to a
reduction of our regular force in Ireland—forthwith I appre-
hend. The Duke entreats in the strongest manner that
reinforcements of infantry may be sent to him.

Believe me ever
dear Lord Whitworth,
Yours most truly

The Lord Lieutenant.   ROBERT PEEL.

PARIS
Rue de la Paix—Hotel du Montblanc—
July 15th, 1815

DEAR LORD WHITWORTH,

AS I owe my trip to Paris in great measure to the
kindness and readiness with which you dispensed
with my services in Ireland—it is but just that I
should give you some account of my proceedings—Croker,
Fitzgerald and myself left Town on Saturday Morning last
[8th] arrived at Dover that night. I was a little disappointed
to hear that the Tricolor Flag was flying at Calais—However we were determined, perhaps rather rashly—to make
an attempt to land, and sailed the next morning in an
armed schooner—putting the guns below and hoisting a
flag of truce when we got into Calais roads. The Governor
however was inexorable—and positively refused us per-

mission to land. We heard that the white flag was flying at Dunkirk and at Boulogne and the wind favoured for the latter—we made for it. As we passed Vimereux and Ambleteuse we saw the white flag flying there and indeed at every intervening village between Calais and Boulogne. It was late in the evening when we arrived off Boulogne—we could discern that there was a flag hoisted, and on standing in close into the harbour we found it was the Tricolor.

Fitzgerald and I were so sick and heartily tired of our voyage, that we resisted most strenuously Croker's proposition to make for Dieppe—we wrote a very civil note to the Commandant—hoisted our flag of Truce and despatched a messenger. He was detained about three hours—he said that our arrival in the roads had caused great alarm in the garrison—that he had been placed under arrest on his landing—had been taken to the Commandant who was holding a sort of Council of war—that the flag of truce was mistaken for the white flag—particularly as the Schooner was armed—and unfortunately for us three or four English Brigs were in the offing.

However he brought with him a civil answer from the Commandant informing us that " une mesure de sureté militaire l'occupoit à le moment," but when he was at leisure he would send a boat for us.

We were half afraid to trust ourselves to him, particularly as he told our envoy that he could not recognize a flag of truce in an armed vessel, but the apprehension of a sail to Dieppe with a contrary wind overcame the apprehension of a day or two's confinement at Boulogne. The boat arrived— and we landed at Boulogne about 3 o'clock on Monday morning. The Commandant was civil to us but did not conceal from us that he was a furious Bonapartist. He said he had no soldiers—if he had 30 that white flag in the next village should not be hoisted—or there should be a massacre if it was. We proceeded on our journey about 7 o'clock on the morning of Monday—nothing could exceed the apparent devotion of all the inhabitants of the country through which we passed to the cause of Louis—the white flag was hanging from every window. Vive le Roi was in every mouth. We met with no interruption until we arrived at Montreuil—where there was a strong garrison—the Commandant like the officers—determined Bonapartists. We had nothing but Castlereagh's passport except La Chatre's which was worse than nothing, but the Commandant allowed us after some parley to proceed. The presence of the military was hardly sufficient to keep down the popular feeling in favour of the King—among the inhabitants it was universal here as every where else, there was not a single exception. At Abbeville we were again stopped. Here there was a very strong garrison—2000 men. Party spirit was running very high. The inhabitants were armed—the military seemed disposed to resist the order which they expected to receive on the day of our arrival, to lay down their arms and leave the town.

Every precaution was taken as if the town was besieged. There were soldiers at every drawbridge. The Commandant however allowed us to proceed—and we arrived safely at Paris on the evening of Tuesday.

Sunday, 16th.

Paris is surrounded by the troops of the allies and nothing can be more interesting than the present situation of it. The streets are crowded with officers and soldiers of all nations. Cossacks—Russians—Prussians, Austrians, Hungarians, etc. The English are great favourites. The Prussians held in the greatest detestation. If they had entered Paris alone—or if the Crowned Heads had delayed their entry—they, the Prussians would probably have pillaged Paris. They have taken some pictures from the Louvre—a very few, however, and none to which they had not some claim. They have demanded the payment of one hundred millions of francs from the city and at this moment—there are Prussian guards in the houses of Perigaux and some of the other principal bankers who are held as a sort of hostage—for the payment of the contribution.

We drove to-day to the Depot d'Artillerie, and were told by the sentry—one of the national guards, that we were welcome to see the salon—but that the Prussians had removed everything which it contained—the sword of Joan of Arc—the knife of Ravaillac—Turenne's sword. I am sorry for this—not on account of the mortification which it will inflict on French vanity—but because I fear the return of the King will be less popular—than it would have been if he could have preserved entire at least those national monuments and relics which are exclusively French.

We paid a visit to Denon the other day. He had some Prussians quartered upon him, and was very loud in his exclamations against *ce* [sic] *bête féroce* as he called Blucher. He expressed his sentiments very freely on political subjects —said the King was not destined to govern France in times like these—and predicted a short duration to his dynasty. He spoke in terms of great and apparently sincere affection towards Bonaparte—he was the last person who saw him before he quitted Paris. Denon observed that he had committed a great error after the battle of Waterloo in quitting the army—that he had by that step lost its confidence—that he ought either to have remained with it— or to have returned to it immediately. If he had summoned the two chambers, informed them without reserve of his disasters and concluded by stating that his travelling carriage was at the door and that he was going to resume the command of the army, that even still he need not have despaired of ultimate success.

At the Tuileries after mass there was a great collection of Marshals—Peers of France—and other rogues of the higher order. We saw Marmont—Macdonald—Masséna —St. Cyr—Dupont, etc., and almost all the General officers of the French army who are in Paris—and did not take a decided part against the King. The garden of the Tuileries was absolutely full of people, and nothing can exceed or describe the enthusiasm of the women and children in favour of the King. If shouts—and applause and Vive le Roi—and white handkerchiefs could contribute to his strength—his throne would be established on solid foundations, but I do not see that men—fighting men—partake so much of the general joy—I confess I think the King has been ill advised in making Fouché his chief confidant and minister. It seems to me that it must preclude him from punishing treason in others—if he rewards so notorious a traitor as Fouché so highly. Fouché betrayed the King— then he betrayed Bonaparte—then he betrayed the Pro-

visional Government of which he was the head and now he is
minister. In fact he betrayed the Provisional Government
deliberately—and on condition that he should be the King's
adviser. The virulence of French traitors—owing to the
impunity of Treason—is beyond conception. Grouchy has
written a letter to the Emperor of Russia requesting him
to intercede in his favour with the King—and to procure for
him permission to retain his rank as Marshal in the French
army or, if that cannot be granted, that the Emperor will
allow him to enter the Russian army retaining his present
rank. The Emperor's answer was not amiss. He had
nothing to say to his first Proposition—and with respect to
his second—it was an indispensable qualification in a Russian
officer that he should be a man of honour.

Pray remember me very kindly to the Duchess of Dorset
and believe me ever

Dear Lord Whitworth,

His Excellency   Yours most truly
The Lord Lieutenant.   ROBERT PEEL.

PARIS, *Monday, July* 17*th.*
Arbuthnot saw Mr. Lane about an hour since I had this
account from him—½ past 3.

Mr. Lane of No. 5 Essex Court in the Temple states
himself to have arrived to-day from France; and he gives
the following account :

That on the 20th he left Paris, and notwithstanding there
were firing of guns and other marks of rejoicing, there was a
general feeling in the town that all was not going well ; that
at Boulogne Mr. Lane saw the *Moniteur* of the 22nd which
gives a long account of what is called the battle of Marennart,
stating that the British were 90,000 men and the French not
so many, that until four in the Evening the French had completely won the battle, but that about that hour the English
Cavalry had attacked the Cuirrassiers and routed them, that
the young guards coming to their assistance got entangled
in their confusion, and the old guard was likewise
" *entrainée.*" At this moment some *Malveillant* in the army
cried " Sauve qui peut " and a general flight commenced;
the whole left wing of the army *dispersed* : He lost all his

214

cannon caissons etc. Buonaparte had ordered the wreck of his army to be collected near Phillipville, and he had issued directions calling on the Northern provinces to rise in mass. This, says the *Moniteur*, ended a battle so glorious yet so fatal to the French arms. Buonaparte has arrived in Paris on the morning of the 21st. The Council of Ministers and the two chambers had been placed in a state of permanency and it was declared high treason to vote an adjournment.

𝕰𝖝𝖙𝖗𝖆𝖈𝖙 of a letter from the DUKE *of* WELLINGTON
to SIR CHARLES FLINT.
dated BRUSSELS.
19 *June* 1815.

What do you think of the total defeat of Bonaparte by the British Army ?

Never was there in the annals of the World so desperate or so hard fought an action, or such a defeat. It was really the battle of the Giants.

My heart is broken by the terrible loss I have sustained of my old friends and companions and my poor Soldiers ; and I shall not be satisfied with this Battle however glorious, if it does not of itself put an end to Bonaparte.

[I have been asked for so many Copies of this (all of which I have refused) that I am glad to return it.]

19 *June* 1815.

On the 16th to the very great astonishment of everyone the French attacked us or rather the Prussians, Lord Wellington came up with a very few Troops including the 7 Divisions and succeeded in stopping them, the next day was passed in partial Cavalry actions and yesterday was fought the severest battle that I believe ever has been known, the disproportion was immense so much so that altho' we constantly repulsed them yet had not the Prussians come up at 7 (altho' in fact they might have been up long before) we perhaps might ultimately have been annihilated. Trotter and I was on the field at the beginning and I count it as the best day of my life—I was there also to-day—the French have abandoned everything—In point of Artillery it is a second Vittoria.

Our loss is so great that our Army will not I fear be in a state to act efficiently—but as we have done the material thing, the Allies may do the rest—the French Cavalry which was very fine suffered beyond expression—For a mile the road is actually strewed with Cuirasses—when I say this, I do not exaggerate. The Prussians are pursuing as fast as they can and with a large body of Troops. There will not be a stop by possibility till we get over the Frontier, after that time I dare not prophesy, but I do not think they will like to attack us again.

The Action was fought in front of *Waterloo* where two Roads separate—the one going to Nivelle, the other to Genappe—the position which was a very beautiful one was in front of the junction of the two roads. [*unsigned.*]

NIVELLE. 19 *June* 1815.

The great action of yesterday was the severest contest either Frenchmen or Englishmen ever witnessed—it was the most obstinate struggle of two brave and rival Nations each firm in its cause—The gallantry of the French could only be exceeded by the resolution and intrepidity of John Bull. It raged from 11 till 9 and was once nearly lost. The Duke seconded by his Troops repaired every momentary disaster.

Buonaparte placed himself at the head of his guards and led them on. The 1st Guards defeated them and put them to the rout and then the dismay became general—The Guards and generally the Infantry were the mainstay of the Action. Our Brigade had the defence of a Post which if lost, lost all. Our Light Company under Colonel Macdonnell were there, the Coldstreams then went down and we held it to the last, tho' the Houses were in Flames. The loss has been immense —The French are totally defeated.

There never was a more severe Battle than that of the 18th. I enclose a little Sketch of it. The dotted Line from Braine la Leud to above La Haye is the brow of the Hills occupied by the Duke of Wellington. The Troops had bivouaced just in the rear. The other dotted line near La Belle Alliance marks the brow of the Hills from where the French attack was made. There are two small Hedges in the Rear of this one. The Attack on Hougomont was very severe from a little before 12 to half past one. Bonaparte then moved a strong Force (continuing however his first Attack for several hours) to attack the left of the Centre where Picton and Ponsonby were killed. He drove our people from the Hedges a short distance but they soon returned and drove him considerably beyond those Hedges. In the Evening he collected a very great force near La Haye Sainte and attacked the Right of the Centre. This was done repeatedly by Infantry and Cavalry but though they frequently got through the Line they could never drive them from their position. The British Artillery was a little in front. The Duke several times left the Guns taking away the Horses and Ammunition, but his Fire was too heavy for the Enemy to bring up Horses to take them off and he as often regained them. At about 7 o'clock the French were heartily sick of it and retired rapidly. The Duke immediately changed his Defensive operations to that of Attack and at the same time Bulow brought up about 30,000 fresh Troops on the right flank of the Enemy near the Village of La Haye. Blucher was also near at hand.

The Rout at this time was complete. The Pursuit was rapid and I really believe that the following morning the French Army had not 50 Guns out of 300 and no Baggage of any sort.

The latter part of this Account I take from others and from seeing the Field of Battle two days afterwards. The first and second attacks I was present at.

The Returns are arrived of Killed and Wounded. The British and Hanoverians lost on the 16th, 17th and 18th 845 Officers and 13,000 Men. The French lost much more. The Method in which the Duke received the united Charges of Cavalry and attacks of Infantry is not common. He formed two Regiments in Squares and united them by a Regt. in Line four deep making a Sort of Curtain between two Bastions. [*unsigned.*]

§ iii

After Lord Whitworth's term of office had come to an end he and the duchess returned to live at Knole, and to make such improvements there as were agreeable to the taste of the early nineteenth century. Such were the Gothic windows of the Orangery, which replaced the Tudor ones and were inscribed with the date 1823, and further changes were projected, such as a design which was to sweep away the symmetry of the lawns on the garden front and bring a curving path up to the house. This scheme, however, was never carried out. The bowling-green still rises, square and formal, backed by the two great tulip trees and the more distant woods of the park. The long perspective of the herbaceous borders was left undisturbed. The apple-trees in the little square orchards, that bear their blossom and their fruit from year to year with such countrified simplicity in the heart of all that magnificence, were not uprooted. Consequently the garden, save for one small section where the paths curve in meaningless scollops among the rhododendrons, remains to-day very much as Anne Clifford knew it. It has, of course, matured. The white rose which was planted under James I's room has climbed until it now reaches beyond his windows on the first floor; the great lime has drooped its branches until they have layered themselves in the ground of their own accord and grown up again with fresh roots into three complete circles all sprung from the parent tree, a cloister of limes, which in summer murmurs like one enormous bee-hive; the magnolia outside the Poets' Parlour has grown nearly to the roof, and bears its mass of flame-shaped blossoms like a giant candelabrum; the beech hedge is twenty feet high; four centuries have winnowed the faultless turf. In spring the wisteria drips its fountains over the top of the wall into the park. The soil is rich and deep and old. The garden has been a garden for four hundred years.

And here, save for a few very brief notes to bring the history of the house down to the present day, these sketches must cease. The duchess Arabella Diana dying in 1825, her estate devolved upon her two daughters, Mary and Elizabeth. Elizabeth, my great-grandmother, who married John West, Lord de la Warr, and who died in 1870, left Buckhurst to her elder sons and Knole to her younger sons, one of whom was my grandfather. He was, as I remember him, a queer and silent old man. He knew nothing whatever about the works of art in the house; he spent hours gazing at the flowers, followed about the garden by two grave demoiselle cranes; he turned his back on all visitors, but sized them up after they had gone in one shrewd and sarcastic phrase; he bore a really remarkable resemblance to the portraits of the old Lord Treasurer, and he seemed to me, with his taciturnity and the never-mentioned background of his own not unromantic past, to stand conformably at the end of the long line of his ancestors. He and I, who so often shared the house alone between us, were companions in a shy and undemonstrative way. Although he had nothing to say to his unfortunate guests, he could understand a child. He told me that there were underground caves in the Wilderness, and I believed him to the extent of digging pits among the laurels in the hope of chancing upon the entrance; he made over a tall tree to me for my own, and I mounted a wooden cannon among its branches to keep away intruders. When I was away, which was seldom, he would write me harlequin letters in different coloured chalks. When I was at home he would put after dinner a plate of fruit for my breakfast into a drawer of his writing-table labelled with my name, and this he never once failed to do, even though there might have been thirty people to dinner in the Great Hall, who watched, no doubt with great surprise, the old man who had been so rude to his neighbours at dinner going unconcernedly round with a plate, picking out the reddest cherries, the bluest grapes, and the ripest peach.

When we were at Knole alone together I used to go down to his sitting-room in the evening to play draughts with him—and never knew whether I played to please him, or he played to please me—and sometimes, very rarely, he told me stories of when he was a small boy, and played with the rocking-horse, and of the journeys by coach with his father and mother from Buckhurst to Knole or from Knole to London; of their taking the silver with them under the seat; of their having outriders with pistols; and of his father and mother never addressing each other, in their children's presence, as anything but " my Lord " and " my Lady." I clasped my knees and stared at him when he told me these stories of an age which already seemed so remote, and his pale blue eyes gazed away into the past, and suddenly his shyness would return to him and the clock in the corner would begin to wheeze in preparation to striking the hour, and he would say that it was time for me to go to bed. But although our understanding of one another was, I am sure, so excellent, our rare conversations remained always on similar fantastic subjects, nor ever approached the intimate or the personal.

Then he fell ill and died when he was over eighty, and became a name like the others, and his portrait took its place among the rest, with a label recording the dates of his birth and death.

APPENDIX

A Note on Thieves' Cant

THE vocabulary given on page 135 contributes no word which may not be found in any cant dictionary, and therefore may appear undeserving of inclusion. But I put it in because I think few people, apart from students of philology, realize the existence of that large section of our language in use among the vagabond classes. Cant and slang, to most people's minds, are synonymous, but this is an error of belief: slang creeps from many sources into the river of language, and so mingles with it that in course of time many use it without knowing that they do so; cant, on the other hand, remains definite and obscure of origin. Slang is loose, expressive, and metaphorical; cant is tight and correct: it has even a literature of its own, broad and racy, incomprehensible to the ordinary reader without the help of a glossary. Its words, for the most part, bear no resemblance to English words; unlike slang, they are not words adapted, for the sake of vividness, to a use for which they were not originally intended, but are applied strictly to their peculiar meaning.

Although the origin of cant as a separate jargon or language is obscure—it does not appear in England till the second half of the sixteenth century—the origin of certain of its words may be traced. Of those included in the vocabulary on page 135, for example, *ken*, for house, comes from *khan* (gipsy and Oriental); *fogus*, for tobacco, comes from *fogo*, an old word for stench; *maund*, or *maunder*, to beg, does not derive, as might be thought, from *maung*, to beg, a gipsy word taken from the Hindu, but from the Anglo-Saxon *mand*, a basket; *bouse*, to drink (which, of

Q

course, has given us booze, with the same meaning, and which in the fourteenth century was perfectly good English), comes from the Dutch *buyzen*, to tipple. *Abram*, naked, is found as *abrannoi*, with the same meaning, in Hungarian gipsy ; *cassan*, cheese, is *cas* in English gipsy ; *dimber* survives for " pretty " in Worcestershire. *Cheat* appears frequently in cant as a common affix.

As for *autem mort*, I find it in an early authority thus defined : " These *autem morts* be married women, as there be but a few. For *autem* in their language is a church, so she is a wife married at the church, and they be as chaste as a cow I have, that goeth to bull every moon, with what bull she careth not."

INDEX

223

INDEX

INDEX

INDEX

INDEX

INDEX

INDEX

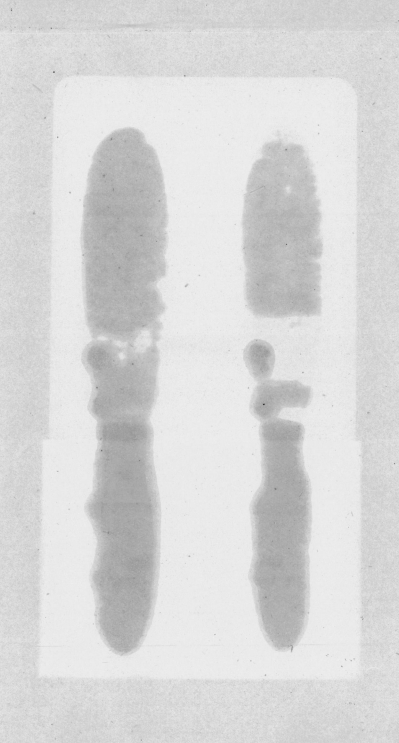

DATE DUE

GAYLORD   PRINTED IN U.S.A.